PLANNING

FOR

EXCELLENCE

How To
Position and Fund
Rehabilitation
and Education Programs

James P. Gelatt, PhD
Director, Sponsored Programs
American Speech-Language-Hearing Association
Rockville, Maryland

AN ASPEN PUBLICATION®
Aspen Publishers, Inc.
Rockville, Maryland
1989

Library of Congress Cataloging-in-Publication Data

Gelatt, James P.
Planning for excellence: how to position and fund
rehabilitation and education programs/James P. Gelatt
p. cm.
"An Aspen publication."
Includes bibliographies and index.
ISBN: 0-8342-0091-0
1. Education and fund raising--United States. I. Title.
LB2336.G45   1989   379.1′3′0973--dc20   89-34495
CIP

Editorial Services: Ruth Bloom

Library of Congress Catalog Card Number: 89-34495
ISBN: 0-8342-0091-0

Printed in the United States of America

1 2 3 4 5

For My Parents

Table of Contents

Preface

Life never was a series of easy victories (not even a series of hard victories). We can't win every round or arrive at a neat solution to every problem. But driving, creative effort to solve problems is the breath of life, for a civilization or an individual.

John W. Gardner
No Easy Victories

IS THIS BOOK FOR YOU?

Is this you?

- Your program is not reaching its potential. But if you had the chance, you could really make something of it.
- Other programs—some right within your own organization—are viewed as successful, and yet you know they're no better than the one you've put together.
- There are projects you'd like to undertake—if you could find a way to come up with the funds.
- You'd like to know more about how to secure funds, but you really don't see yourself as a fund-raiser.
- The administration doesn't seem to understand how valuable your program could be, and frankly you're more than a little concerned about its future.

Sound at all familiar? Then maybe this book is for you.

This book is intended to help you

- decide where you want your program to go and how to get there
- become "literate" regarding some useful tools, thereby taking the mystery out of marketing, planning, and resource development
- choose among options—what works best for you and the environment in which you live and work
- understand the interrelationship between planning and success (without the former, the latter is very unlikely)

You don't have to become a strategic planner to be a success. You don't have to get a degree in marketing. And you don't have to start a second career as a fund-raiser.

So What Do You Need?

You need to be serious about improving your program. Doing anything well takes time. Planning. Commitment.

The first commitment should be to yourself. You've got to accept that it's OK to let go and dream a bit. For your program to grow, it will be necessary to overcome some common obstacles:

- the desire to let things stay as they are
- the failure to see what your real strengths are
- the propensity to remain bound by what has been done before
- the fear of appearing too aggressive
- the tendency to prejudge the outcome

The writer Isaac Bashevis Singer once noted, "If you keep on saying things are going to be bad, you have a good chance of being a prophet." This book is based on the reverse of that premise: You can positively influence your future if you believe you can.

You may have to take some chances. But you can hedge your bets. You'll know best when it's time to involve others, when to "go public" with your ideas.

For now, you will lose nothing by letting go.

WHAT THIS BOOK IS AND IS NOT

Warning: There is an underlying premise at work throughout this text, namely, that it is possible to have a significant measure of control over your program's future. You cannot control every variable, but you can do a great deal to make yours into the model program you'd like it to be.

A Tutorial for Students

In *No Easy Victories*, John Gardner has this to say about the role of universities:

We need in the university community a focused, systematic, responsible, even aggressive concern for the manner in which society is evolving—a concern for its values, for the problems it faces, and for the strategies appropriate to clarify those values and to solve those problems.

We need [men and women] who are seeking new solutions and helping us on toward those solutions. We need designers of the future.[1]

This text is designed to provide students with a *focused* look at how to develop a successful program—hence the concept of a tutorial. It offers a set of skills that few of us ever develop until well into our careers. The goal is to provide individuals completing graduate study with the means to respond to the various challenges they will encounter when they enter the world of full-time work.

As a course text, the book provides an opportunity for both intensive classroom discussion and individual endeavor. The chapter on trends, for example, can be used in conjunction with an assignment requiring students to develop potential solutions to the problems that we will all face in the coming decade.

A Workshop in Print

This text has also been designed to function at the in-service level as a "workshop in print." It is laid out for you to use as if you were attending a workshop on "How to Make Your Program a Success."

It is structured so that you can begin and complete each chapter within a discrete time period (defined by you). It is also generally sequential (planning comes before doing, having something to say comes before going public, and so on).

Why a workshop in print? Because you need to get into the same frame of mind that you get into when you go to a workshop, especially one out of town. At a workshop, you're away from your desk, your phone, and your appointment calendar. That gives you a chance to focus on a single subject for a decent amount of time, a chance to really begin to understand it.

Think about a topic you first became familiar with by attending a workshop. The use of computers, for example. You set aside the time for intensive "hands-on" training. For that period of a few days, you became a student again in order to learn something of value.

That is what is being asked of you here. In order to get the full benefit of this book, you need to make the same kind of commitment, a commitment to set aside the time and to do the exercises. So before you go to Chapter 2, decide how to structure your schedule so that you can dedicate a period of time every week to attend this workshop in print free from outside pressures.

You may even decide that you want to take some time off in order to concentrate on what you read. Or you may find that it's sufficient to go to the library, close your door, or study the book at home. Whatever. The point is that this book is to be used, not simply read. Before you get deeply into it, you need to consider how you will carve out blocks of time. One comment sometimes heard at workshops is, "I figure if I come away with one useful new idea, it's been worth my time." You may have said that yourself.

Think of it: one idea, purchased at the cost of a workshop involving a considerable investment of funds and time. What is proposed here is something else again—not just a few good ideas but a chance to make your program what you would like it to be. However, the commitment on your part needs to be correspondingly great.

Two Notes

Note One: It may be helpful to begin compiling your thoughts in one common place. This may be a loose-leaf workshop notebook divided into sections corresponding to the major sections of this book. Or it may be a computer disk dedicated just to the activities in this book (with individual files corresponding to the major sections). The important thing is to have it all together, each part building on the one before. It's also important to be able to make changes and additions easily as ideas come to you.

Note Two: The word program *is used throughout this text* for any entity (e.g., a department, division, or unit) contained within a larger organization or institution. For *program*, read whatever your own defined unit is called.

What This Book Is Not

This is not a workbook on how to use "smoke and mirrors," on how to create the illusion of a good program where one does not exist. It is intended to give you the opportunity to make your program what it can be—by allowing you to see how others have succeeded and to apply the same principles that were used.

What can you achieve?

1. a sound reputation (within your own community and perhaps beyond)
2. the ability to attract funds

3. recognition from others that your program makes a positive contribution to the organization and is important to the organization's mission
4. the ability to keep your program in the forefront by identifying new challenges and responding to them quickly

---

NOTE

1. John W. Gardner, *No Easy Victories*, ed. Helen Rowan (New York: Harper & Row, 1968), 87.

Chapter 1

Setting the Stage

The greatest waste of our natural resources is the number of people who never achieve their potential. . . . Reputations are made by searching for things that can't be done and doing them.

United Technologies Corporation

We are living in an age of limits. Those of us who grew up during the Kennedy era or Johnson's Great Society can recall with nostalgia a time when there always seemed to be sufficient funds to get done whatever we wanted. Whether we were on a college campus or in a nonprofit clinic or other institution, since it was a period of growth, it was easier to expand programs and staff and facilities.

By contrast, many programs are now in a period of retrenchment. Our administrators are looking for ways to cut costs. Our deans are charged with finding programs and departments that can be trimmed. Positions that become vacant are sometimes left unfilled, and departments that have been judged nonessential become nonexistent.

Simply stated, with the continuing decline in funds readily available, with retrenchment occurring in health and education settings, those of us whose programs are not perceived as successful may find ourselves without a program—or with one that is quite unlike the one we want.

SUCCESS IN AN AGE OF LIMITS

And yet there are programs, and we can all point to at least one, that continue to prosper, adding staff, expanding facilities, and gaining in reputation. How do the leaders of such programs do it? And why can't you?

Perhaps you can.

What Makes a Program a Success?

You need first to consider what it is that makes a program a success in the eyes of others. A "successful" program probably possesses at least the following qualities:

- It has a local reputation, if not a regional or national reputation, as an outstanding program. The services that it provides are considered "model."
- It attracts funds, not only for itself but for the institution in which it is housed.
- It is viewed as an integral part of the overall organization and as a program that provides services among the most important.
- It always seems to be one step ahead of other programs, both in the organization and in others like it.

The most certain observation that one can make about successful programs is this: They have determined what they can do well, they have found the means to do what they do well, and they are able to demonstrate their success to others.

Put another way, good programs do not come about by accident. While it may evolve, each good program reflects the vision and determination of at least one person who has influenced its destiny. Such people, implicitly if not explicitly, will have implemented a plan that has gotten the program where it is and that will get it further. Their planning has taken into account not only what goal they would like to attain and how to attain it, but also who needs to "buy into" that goal and know of their work if they are to succeed.

MAKING YOURS A SUCCESSFUL PROGRAM

Call it "marketing," "planning," "positioning"—what this book is about is how to make your program outstanding.

How? By determining what it is you want your program to become and devising a practicable course of action that takes into account the realities of your organization.

For a program to become successful and remain so, it must integrate each of the following four ingredients: planning, resources, visibility, and leadership. As indicated in Figure 1-1, these elements are interdependent.

1. Start with a *plan*. If you don't have time to plan, you don't have time to succeed.
2. Even with a sound plan, you will find it difficult at best to make your program successful without adequate *resources*.
3. You will also probably find it difficult to garner those resources without developing an image of potential, if not actual, success (in other words, *visibility*).
4. Conversely, no program will long be viewed as successful without being able to demonstrate *leadership*. Without such a demonstration, resources for the program will diminish.

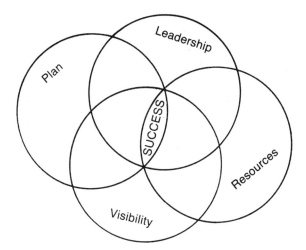

Figure 1-1 The Elements of a Successful Program

The four elements of success correspond to the parts of this book. Part I is dedicated to developing the plan, and Part II to gathering the resources (through the process of development). Part III shows how to create the kind of visibility that will facilitate acquisition of resources. The final part addresses the question of leadership.

USING BUSINESS TOOLS IN NONPROFIT SETTINGS

The central approach presented in this book is to apply concepts of marketing to the two elements essential to making your program a success: planning and development.

1. Planning includes
   - understanding trends
   - evaluating your program's and institution's potential
   - laying out goals, objectives, and a course of action
   - determining how best to implement the plan given the variables unique to your institution
2. Development involves putting that plan into operation through
   - implementing activities that will provide your program with financial support from the public or private sector
   - "positioning" your program in such a way that it is in a favorable position to succeed
   - developing your own skills as a leader of what will become a very successful program

While marketing has been a foundation of business for decades and increasingly a tool of nonprofit organizations, there is little in print about the use of marketing at the departmental level within the university, hospital, or other setting, and even less about the use of marketing to obtain the support necessary to implement good ideas. For these reasons, it might be useful to review briefly some of the principles behind marketing as they relate to the nonprofit world.

Marketing Defined

The goal of marketing is to effect an exchange: You have a service to offer; I have a desire for that service and some money to spend for it. We make a trade—hopefully to our mutual satisfaction.

There are certain principles fundamental to this trade, principles which need to be inculcated in order to have this process of trade, of exchange, occur more or less regularly and dependably. These principles include the following:[1]

- Marketing begins with planning—identifying what a certain public might want and then developing a means to provide it.
- The approach is systematic rather than random. If you decide to offer a product or service, it is in the context of an overall schema or set of goals.
- You need to provide the setting in which voluntary exchanges will take place. You want clients to choose your program; you want funders to do the same.
- What you have to offer will not be of interest to everyone. You need to identify the segments of the population that might have an interest in using your services, buying your products, or financially supporting your ability to provide such services and products to others.
- If you are to attract others, if you are to effect an exchange of what they can offer for what you can provide, you need to think in terms not only of what they might want but of what they are in a position to demand by virtue of their ability to pay for it.
- "Marketing is user-oriented, not seller-oriented."[2]

Marketing, because it is user-oriented, probably constitutes a departure from the way that you think about yourself. Although you will continue to be an educator or clinician, thinking in marketing terms requires that you recognize that your role—if you are to survive and to thrive—is both initiatory and responsive. It is initiatory inasmuch as it requires digging to find out what needs and desires exist. It is responsive inasmuch as it requires

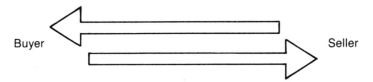

Figure 1-2 Marketing Paradigm: For-Profit Organization

developing a means to meet those needs and desires in a way that is compatible with your own perceived raison d'etre.

As indicated in Figure 1-2, in the business world the exchange is two-way: You have a car; I both want it and have the means to acquire it. In the nonprofit world, an additional party often comes into play, be it a third party reimburser or an outside source of funding via a grant or similar mechanism (Figure 1-3).

In this book, we will focus on outside sources of funding and how a program can expand or enrich what it does by garnering financial support from the public or private sector. Why?

1. Obtaining outside funding provides tremendous opportunities that would not otherwise exist.
2. Third party reimbursement may well be largely beyond the control of a program director. Obtaining grant funding or similar support need not be.

Marketing Goals

There are basically four reasons to use marketing:[3]

1. You want to broaden the degree to which your products or services are used by others. For example, you know you have a sound clinical program, but you need to develop the means of letting others know of it—and perhaps secure the funding to expand what you do.

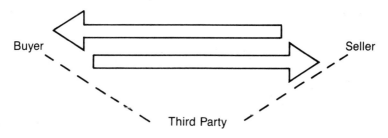

Figure 1-3 Marketing Paradigm: Nonprofit Organization

2. You want to improve the way people who use your services feel about them. Your educational program is good, but it could be better. Marketing provides some of the tools to improve people's attitudes.
3. You want to expand the range of services which you can offer. You have an excellent preservice educational program but do almost nothing in the way of in-service training. You have a dynamic program for children with learning disabilities but not anything for adults who have learning disabilities and need coping skills.
4. You want to improve the quality of life of those who come into contact with you by providing greater access to your services in more pleasant, modern settings and at a fair, reasonable cost.

Considering the above, it should be clear that marketing is no longer foreign to the traditional nonprofit philosophy. It is, rather, a set of strategies that can enable you to do more of what you do well. Christopher Smith, in *Marketing Rehabilitation Facility Products and Services*, presents a somewhat longer, although clearly related, set of reasons for undertaking marketing:

- to insure survival
- to develop a positive image
- to develop services and structures
- to be responsive to the public
- to check on long- and short-range planning objectives
- to provide service to identified customers
- to develop strategies to handle competition
- to allow the facility to plan for expanding operations
- to permit the organization to adapt to changes in technology
- to assist in assuring productiveness
- to improve financial stability
- to prepare the organization for change[4]

Principles of Marketing in the Nonprofit World

Following are the key principles of a marketing approach.

1. Analyze opportunities. As will be discussed in the chapters on trends, planning, and making decisions, a first step is to give some thought to new directions that your program might take based on a look at emerging trends. You can begin to develop possible program initiatives that will respond to needs and desires in a way that will better your program and its image.

2. Look within. You should also consider the strengths and weaknesses of your own program and of the institution in which it is housed. Further, you will need to evaluate possible constraints that must be addressed if you are to pursue new opportunities.

3. Develop specific approaches. These will include both activities that are program-related and strategies to obtain the necessary support. In marketing terminology, you will create the "market mix." The mix includes the four P's: place (where you want to provide new services or products), products (services, materials, publications, and so on), price (what it will cost you to move into new areas), and promotion (making the services or products known).

4. Select your targets. Part of the process of determining place involves segmenting the market: narrowing your vision to focus on those individuals who are most likely to want what it is you have to offer, be they students, clients, or potential funders.

5. Make yourself known. In the chapter entitled "Visibility," we will consider how to improve your chances for success by influencing how and in what contexts others think of you.

The goal of this book is to help you—whether you are completing a course of study or active within your own profession—develop the kind of program that you know is possible. And hopefully have some fun along the way.

NOTES

1. The explication of marketing principles draws on the work of Philip Kotler in *Marketing for Nonprofit Organizations* (Englewood Cliffs, N.J.: Prentice-Hall, 1975), 3–7.

2. Ibid., 7.

3. These reasons are based on the goals of marketing stated by Philip Kotler and Gary Armstrong in *Marketing: An Introduction* (Englewood Cliffs, N.J.: Prentice-Hall, 1987), 18–19.

4. Christopher A. Smith and Goodwill Industries of America, Inc., *Marketing Rehabilitation Facility Products and Services* (Menomonie, Wisc.: University of Wisconsin-Stout, School of Education and Human Services, Stout Vocational Rehabilitation Institute, 1987), 3–4.

Part I

Planning

Before you can score, you must first have a goal.

Greek Proverb

Make no little plans. They have no magic . . . and probably will not be realized. Make big plans; aim high in hope and work. . . . Remember that when you create a situation that captures the imagination, you capture life, reason, everything.

Daniel H. Burnham
Accent on Philanthropy II

In the context of this workshop in print, for "planning" read "strategic planning." Strategic planning involves envisioning a desired future and developing a working plan to guide the program into that future. Having decided where you want to go, you can then develop strategies that help point the way. "In the simplest of terms, it requires doing the right things, at the right times, and most important of all, for the right reasons."* Good planning is thus nothing less than strategic thinking.

Effective planning is the point of convergence of certain interrelated activities:

1. studying trends that could or will impact your program or that might make it reasonable to develop new projects
2. recognizing what it is you do well as a department or unit and as an organization and where you have limitations
3. articulating your purpose (describing, in marketing terms, what business you are in and what product lines and services you have to offer)
4. setting out measurable objectives and a course of action
5. laying out your case for support (who you are, the projects you want to undertake, and what will be required)

Each of these key activities will be addressed in turn in the chapters that follow.

What are the goals of this planning?

1. to develop new ideas and new approaches that both merit support and will become the measures by which your program is evaluated
2. to gain a competitive edge
3. to create the kind of program that you know is possible

---

*Peter R. Johnson, *Strategic Thinking* (Newport Beach, Calif.: Johnson & Company, n.d.): 31.

Chapter 2

Making Some Decisions

The more faithfully you listen to the voice within you, the better you will hear what is sounding outside.

Dag Hammarskjold
Markings

Can you imagine what you would like your program to look like, if all went well, five years from now? In our first workshop session, we're going to develop that picture.

REVIEW

In Chapter 1 we considered some elements that can help make a successful program. These can be summarized as planning, resources, visibility, and leadership.

1. Planning allows us to determine where we want to go and what steps are necessary to get there.
2. Resources include the funding, personnel, and administrative support that are needed to mount and maintain a successful effort.
3. Visibility is achieved by developing ways of letting others know that they are dealing with a successful program.
4. Leadership depends on the personal qualities that make for successful programs.

FIVE YEARS FROM TODAY

We're going to start by articulating the vision of where you want your program to be in five years. Imagine for a few minutes how you might describe your program to someone who does not know of it—or did five years earlier but has lost touch.

What kind of changes have been made? Where are you housed? What are the size and composition of your staff? What is the type of client or student with whom you work?

Take a few minutes to let yourself dream. Maybe close your eyes, if that helps. Then, on a page or two, write down how you would like to be able to describe your program five years from now.

Is there something you've always wished you could be doing if there were the funds? Take a chance and write it down. Be as specific as you can about the elements that you include. Below are some questions that might be of help.

Staff

How many persons do you have on staff? What are their backgrounds and areas of expertise? What is the range of activities in which they are engaged? How did you attract them to your program? Are their skills concentrated in particular areas (for example, bilingual studies, technology, early childhood training)?

Facilities

Where are you located? Are you in one setting or do you have one central unit with satellite sites? Do you have plans for new facilities? What types of equipment do you have?

Client Populations

What kind of clients, patients, or students do you see in your vision of the future? What has attracted them to your program? Are they drawn entirely from your local area or are there elements of your program that attract people from outside your area? What methods of recruitment do you employ?

Constituencies

With whom do you interact within your institution, within the community, or at a state, regional, or national level? Do you have any regular contact with other programs similar to yours? With public schools? What is your relationship with local area employers? With adult learners?

Your Role

What is your own role in all of this? Do you essentially have the same role that you have today? In the same institution? Have you undertaken some new activities—writing, teaching, or consulting—in the five years that have elapsed?

Having Trouble?

Are you having difficulties with this exercise? Afraid it doesn't seem useful to you?

If so, ask yourself the following questions. Have you reached your full potential? Is your program everything you would like it to be? It might interest you to know that humans tend to use only about 10 percent of the brain's ability. Ten percent! That means that your staff—and you yourself—have talents that you haven't begun to tap.

Some of the top athletes in the country, athletes who excel because they are closer to reaching their full potential, have discovered an effective tool. Before they run a race, play a football game, throw the shot, they visualize themselves as they would like to be.

In their mind's eye they see themselves finishing that 26th mile feeling strong, breathing well, with enough left for a final "kick." Or they move mentally through key plays in the game. Ball in hand, dodging defenders, they sprint toward the goal line. Or turning, balanced on one foot, they launch the shot, putting it farther than ever before.

They are not daydreaming of their future. They're not simply imagining. They are creating that future in their minds. Thus, when it comes time to create it in actuality, they're ready. They know what's ahead. They've anticipated the challenges. And they have seen the goal.

It works for some of the finest athletes alive. And it can work for you. That's what this session is all about: envisioning what it is you want your program to become and how to get it there.

Take a Break

Every workshop schedules time for breaks, and this is your first one. Whether the exercises in this book are done within a class setting or on your own, it might be helpful to leave what you've written alone for a little while. Overnight, preferably, or until the next class meeting.

Back to Work

Now take another look at it. Anything you would change? Left anything out?

For example, did you say something about the following?

- the physical location of your facility, its size, capability, and so on
- the type or caliber of your staff
- the program's students or clients
- the program's relationship with other key organizational entities (for example, departments, the administration, and so on)
- a new program, a new thrust, something that would really put your program on the map
- your own role five years from now

Again, if there's something you want to add or change, feel free. This is a working document, and you need to feel comfortable with it and be willing to modify it along the way.

At the same time, your vision ought to feel a little scary. If what you've visualized as existing five years hence seems much like what exists now, you may have set your sights too low.

You lose nothing by reaching, especially in an exercise such as this one. You can always scale back. But you'll limit how far you can reach if you start by being unambitious in your dreams.

TAKING CARE OF BUSINESS

What you have now is the basis for a goal, a mission, or a focus for your program. You've attempted to define the business you are in—or want to be in.

Business. If you're not comfortable with that term, now's a good time to become comfortable. For any program to succeed in this age of limits, it must be partly conceived in terms of the "bottom line," in terms of measurable end products.

For years many artistic programs around the country, such as ballet and repertory acting companies, showed early promise but then went under. One reason was that the ballet companies were usually headed up by former dancers, the acting companies by those who had spent their lives on the boards. They had extensive knowledge about their craft, yet virtually no understanding of the business that they were in. There was nothing wrong with the fact that they were dreamers, but their dreams lacked clarity and were never converted into doable strategies. In short, they did not recognize the need to make clear what they wanted to accomplish and then to sell their vision to others who could bring it into reality.

For your program to succeed, you need to better define who you are. This means using some of the planning and management skills required in the business world. You need to recognize that those who have decision-making roles in your institution are increasingly thinking in business terms.

The position formerly called *director of finance* is now often appropriately referred to as *vice president for administration,* and the public relations staff are finding themselves housed in the marketing department.

The "People Business"

However, it is not being suggested that what you do, the business you are in, should be equated with economics. This book is not predicated on developing a system in which decisions are made by the finance division (or whatever is the equivalent in your institution).

You are in the business of people. That's why you chose a career in health or education. What is being suggested is merely that you become more professional. And in order to do that, you need to interlock vision with resources and visibility.

Those artistic programs that went under were filled with men and women of vision. What those people failed to adequately consider was how they were going to get the visibility and the resources which would allow them to realize their dreams.

Thinking Big

Consider for a second what you've said about the business you are in. Have you described it in big enough terms?

- not *physical therapy* or *occupational therapy* but *rehabilitation*
- not *medical technology, radiologic science,* or *cytotechnology* but *diagnosis of illness*
- not *teaching* but *education*
- not *intermediate care* but *quality of life*

Consider what it is you do in terms of what, at your best, you do for others. How you enrich people's lives.

Education is nothing less than preparing the best and brightest to lead the country of tomorrow. It's also helping others to compensate for limitations placed on them. Education is teaching people how to think, how to cope.

Rehabilitation is returning fellow humans to the fullest function that is possible. It's getting them back to where they can be productive, to where they can know again what it is to be father, wife, or friend.

Those of us in the human services, which include all aspects of education and health care delivery, have a tendency to undervalue what we do. It's part of our training to underestimate the results of our research. And it's part of our makeup to change people's lives without giving ourselves credit for it. We need to be more impressed with what we do. We need to become more comfortable talking about it. Because if we're not convinced of the worth of our activities and goals, it'll be almost impossible to share our vision with anyone else.

We have deliberately kept this chapter shorter than most of the ones that follow, because in it you do much of the work. Some of the others will involve more information sharing. This one, placed as it is at the start of our workshop in print, makes some demands on you, and it's important that you have done the suggested exercise before moving on.

Chapter 3

Between Here and There

Know thyself.

Inscription at Delphi

In the previous chapter, we considered the kind of program that we would like ours to become. Get there we will. And the next step in charting a course is to consider where we are now.

FOUR TYPICAL PROGRAM MODELS

Which of the following models seems to best characterize your program today?

Model 1

The first model involves a program that is relatively new to its institution. It may have been created because the institution found that its own range of programs had a gap in it or because it's the kind of program that is cropping up in institutions across the country and that everyone feels his or her organization must have.

Because it is new, it's a relative unknown to the administration and to the other units.

What are some advantages of such a program?

- It was probably created out of a perceived need.
- Because it is new, it might be able to get some things done, to get the administration to agree to some changes, or to garner some resources that a year or two later will be hard to come by.
- It does not have a history of failure, false starts, inability to get along with other units, and cost overruns.

What are some disadvantages?

- It has no track record.

16

- It may be perceived as a threat by other more established units.
- Its resources may be limited.

Model 2

Model 2 involves a program that has existed for a while within the institution but is largely untested and unproven. Its record is neither exemplary nor embarrassing. It therefore does not enjoy a central role in the organization, but neither does it suffer from a history of ill will and "screw ups."

Some advantages:

- Persons within the program are likely to know something about the institution and how it works—who makes decisions, who influences decisions, what the institution's financial picture is, and what has been tried before.
- There are some projects that the program has undertaken with reasonable success, and thus there is the potential for a record to build on.
- Unlike some programs, it probably does not have a lot of enemies. Indeed, it may have some friends, owing to relationships which have been established, projects on which it has worked jointly, or contacts that it has made in the community or elsewhere.

Some disadvantages:

- The program will have to overcome the perception that it is not a leader, not at the center of the organization's focus.
- It may not have attracted the same caliber of staff as similar programs in other institutions, including some that may be in competition.
- It does not have the same kind of backing from the administration that other more impressive units enjoy.

Model 3

The Model 3 program is on shaky ground. The institution is doing some belt tightening. Not only are new personnel positions not being approved, but it is increasingly difficult to replace staff lost through attrition. Indeed, the administration is looking for places where other cuts might be made. The integrity of the department is at risk.

In health settings this may be result in the emergence of the "multiskilled practitioner," that is, someone who can function in diverse roles requiring diverse skills. In education, it may result in a move to consolidate departments (for example, joining curriculum and instruction with education technology or collapsing audiology into otolaryngology).

Advantages:

- As with the Model 2 program, the players know the institution and where and how decisions are made.
- The program has a constituency, made up, for example, of students who have gone through it or clients whom it has served. Its constituency is a resource that can be drawn upon. This is an advantage over the program that is only just beginning.

Disadvantages:

- The program will need to act quickly to develop a course of action that is positive and that the institution will see as beneficial to its financial situation. Time is not necessarily on its side.
- The program is probably not viewed as essential to the mission of the institution. That perception will need to be changed.

Model 4

The Model 4 program has potential but is not in the mainstream of the organization. It may be an outstanding program in occupational therapy, but unfortunately it is housed in an institution dominated by pediatrics. Or it may be an outstanding department of public health, but the administration is much more enthusiastic about the business department: That's the unit that is attracting high-caliber students and lots of them.

Advantages:

- The Model 4 program has established itself. Although it may not be integral to the institution, it is recognized by its peers and those whom it serves and educates.
- There are specific successes which it has achieved. These can be highlighted in proposals, case statements, and rationales developed for the administration.
- The program may have links with its own national association and even be formally accredited or otherwise recognized.
- It has a constituency—students, clients, their families. Some of these people can be called upon for financial and other help.

Disadvantages:

- Any move on the part of the department to expand its program may be viewed with mistrust by those units that are either more central to the institution or would like to be.
- A cogent argument will need to be made demonstrating how the program does in fact contribute to the overall goals of the institution.

GETTING THERE

The question is, How do you get from here to there? How do you get from today's program to where you'd like to be in five years. What is required, among other things, is sound, careful planning.

We'll discuss the particulars of planning in the next chapter. For now, one of the questions that needs to be asked is, What will it take to reach your goal? Said another way, What presently exists that can be drawn on to reach that goal? What strengths can you build upon? What resources are available?

You also have to consider what might keep you from reaching your goal. What challenges exist? What problems?

We'll look at some larger issues and trends later (in Chapter 4). We'll also look at how best to involve other key players (in Chapter 6). But let's begin with a look at some factors that might influence your success.

Problem Areas

Consider the vitality of your local economy, of the economy of your state. Does the economy hinder your chances of getting a new program in place? If so, you'll want to think about alternative funding sources.

What's the general condition of the field you are in? If it's health care, are you affected by consolidation, by the growth of proprietary institutions? Is the service your program offers generally viewed as a moneymaker for an institution like yours?

If you're in higher education, are you too affected by consolidation? Is your department housed within a school that is well respected on campus? Are you finding it difficult to attract quality students?

Resources

Are there other units within your organization with whom you might link up to develop a new project?

What kind of cooperative ventures might be initiated with institutions within your community (for example, public schools, community colleges, or universities)? Is there a rehabilitation facility whose resources you could draw on?

What links could you forge with the local corporations in your area? Could you offer a program to their employees that in turn might provide you with support?

Strengths and Weaknesses

Although you need to look at your "environment," the world that affects your chances of reaching your goal, you also need to look at what your program has to offer.

This might be a good time to involve some other people, such as members of your staff, people who know your program well, and people whom you might want to interest in what you'd like to do. Be selective. What you want is constructive advice from those who will have your best interests at heart.

Ask others what they see as the two or three best features of your program and the two or three worst. (Ask yourself this question as well.)

Note: It might be helpful to set up a section in your workbook or on a computer disk called "Strengths and Weaknesses." List your program's strengths and weaknesses and indicate by "weight" how important each of them is to your overall success. The lists might look like this:

Strengths (Positive Features)	Weight
Well known by business community.	3
Good reputation among pediatricians.	1
. . .	

Suggested Action Steps
Talk with pediatricians about joint project?

Weaknesses (Negative Features)	Weight
Not considered essential program.	1
Reputation largely local.	2
. . .	

Suggested Action Steps
Get involved on national association committee.

The lists can be as long as you want. It's probably best not to attempt to quantify the importance of the items at first; rather, just get them written down. Then go back and indicate some order of importance among them. For example, you might consider how critical the strength or weakness of an item is for success in developing new plans. You could indicate the criticalness by means of a 1–5 rating scale, as is used above.

The good features are the ones you'll want to build on, publicize, and enrich. The bad ones you're going to have to deal with. But then you knew that.

The list of strengths is also going to go into a larger document that you'll be developing. This document, which may be in outline form at first, is for the purpose of presenting a convincing case that your program is worthy of investment. We'll cover the development of this document, called a *case statement,* in Chapter 13. But with this document in mind, you may want to clean up the list of strengths, being sure to use language that someone unfamiliar with your program could understand.

Now about the weaknesses. You need to look at them again in order to separate them into two lists. One list should contain weaknesses that need to be addressed if your vision of what your program can be is to be realized. The other should contain weaknesses that, for whatever reason, are not going to be a priority. They're unimportant overall, you can live with them, they're beyond change—or whatever.

For weaknesses that you decide not to address directly, you will nevertheless need to acknowledge their importance. It's worth being scrupulously and painfully honest about your weaknesses, at least to yourself. They will surely come back to haunt you if you aren't honest.

At the same time, remember that you don't need to be outstanding in every area in order for your program to be a success. Indeed, some very successful programs have effectively narrowed their focus to the extent that they excel in essentially one area.

Make that two areas. First, they have the ability to do something well. Second, they have the ability (and willingness) to let others know about it.

Chapter 4

Pertinent Trends—And What To Do about Them

By failing to prepare, you are preparing to fail.

Benjamin Franklin
Poor Richard's Almanac

Most of us have at one time or another heard a lecture on future trends in which the speaker rattled off impressive statistics on what our country was going to be like in the year 2000 and beyond. Periodicals from *American Demographics* to *USA Today* provide information (maybe more information than we really want) on everything from the graying of America to the reemergence of the picture phone. John Naisbitt, among others, has noted one result: "Running out of information is not a problem, but drowning in it is."[1] To pursue the metaphor, what we need is not more information but a pail, a paddle, and someone to point us toward shore.

That's a tall order. What we'll try to do, in this chapter, is look at some trends and consider realistically why they might be important to you and how you might incorporate them into strategies that you are developing. The chapter will provide a paddle and compass, if you will, but you'll have to supply the pail. (And with that, let's set this metaphor adrift.)

THE FRAMEWORK

Part of the reason why it's usually so hard to make sense of information on trends is that most people haven't provided themselves with a framework in which to sort it and then discard what is unneeded. That framework should consist of the goals that they have set themselves. If this were a small group exercise, we might at this point ask each participant to jot down on a piece of paper or three-by-five card two or three goals that he or she would like to pursue. For example:

- Goal: To become the premier program in the region for children aged 0–2.
- Goal: To build a faculty of established researchers who can attract their own funding.

- Goal: To expand a therapy program into the local community.
- Goal: To be recognized as one of the most successful programs in the institution.

So, before we proceed with this section on trends and how they might affect you, take just a minute and review the goals that you developed in the exercise on visioning, in which you gave thought to what you would like your program to be in five years' time.

Chunking

Chunking is nothing more than taking manageable "bites." It requires that you separate out major pieces of information, group them, and then deal with the groups one group at a time. One way to do this is to establish a folder, pile, or workbook section for each major trend and begin to develop a resource file, tossing in (or on, if you prefer stacks) news clippings, magazines with pages noted, sections from searches of the literature, and information on where to get information (a mailing address for a center on gerontology, for example).

Attitude

One of the problems with the metaphor of being adrift in a sea of information (in addition to its eventual tediousness) is that it expresses the wrong attitude. Trends can and should work for you. But first you need to bury three myths.

Myth #1

"National trends don't make any difference to me. I'm not dealing on a national level. What somebody thinks is going to happen in 1995 is unimportant to my program. We'll be lucky if we have a program by that time."

National trends, even international trends, have a way of impacting all of us at some time and at certain points. For example, in the late 1960s and early 1970s events took place which were later recognized as precursors of the landmark Education for All Handicapped Children Act. Implementation of that act has affected virtually everyone who works in health or education. The signs were there for those who wanted to read them and begin preparing.

The reverse may also be true. Those who choose not to look ahead and have the attitude that "we'll be lucky to have a program by that time" may be doomed to fulfill their own prophecy.

Myth #2

"I try to keep informed about major trends, but frankly much of what I read is just bad news. If anything, given what I see on the horizon, it's going to be harder just to keep what we have in our program. That's what makes long-range planning seem so futile."

Two points are worth making in debunking this myth. First, not all of the news is bad. There are technologies on the way, for example, that will dramatically improve people's ability to make informed decisions, to make correct diagnoses, and to teach others to excel.

Second, even seemingly bad news needs to be faced, and it may, when considered closely, indicate opportunities for new programs. Think how much we have learned about traumatic brain injury, for example, by having to deal with the increase in vehicular accidents.

Myth #3

"Trends are nothing but best guesses. If you asked two 'experts' about what the economy is going to be like five years from now, you'd probably get two different answers."

Keep in mind that we are talking about trends, not predictions, which are admittedly risky (recall the weather forecaster who called for light snow on the day that began the "blizzard of '88"). Trends are more than best guesses. Although we may not know exactly how many people will be over the age of 65 in 1995, it is possible to make some fairly close estimates, close enough to know that the amount of elderly people will impact our lives significantly.

In some areas, the economy being one, there can be little assurance about trends. The implication is not that we ought to ignore them but rather that we ought to develop contingency plans. If the economy improves, that may provide opportunities for support from local companies. If it doesn't, we'll need to look elsewhere—and should be prepared to do so.

MAKING SENSE OF SOME TRENDS

It would now be appropriate to take a look at some trends with an eye to how they might affect your program and what kind of proactive position you might want to take. For example, consider these questions:

- What influence might demographic changes (for example, the aging of the population, the end of the baby boom, more women in the work force) have on what you want to do? Do any such changes offer an opportunity for your program?

- How will you be affected by the increased percentage of minorities in the population?
- What kind of new project could you develop as a response to a certain trend?
- Is there something about a certain trend that might be helpful in better stating what it is that you do?
- In general, how can you use each trend to create an opportunity and how can you then turn each opportunity into a success.

We're Not As Young As We Used To Be

The fact that the average age of Americans is increasing will affect virtually every program from philosophy to physical therapy. There are at least three subsets of this trend that merit further study.

Fewer Children

There will be proportionately fewer children to serve. If your program focuses on school-aged populations, you may find you have less clients or students. It may be necessary to broaden either the age ranges for your program or your catchment area.

No Longer Babies

The baby boom generation is maturing. In 1980 the largest age group consisted of those who were 20–24 years old, followed closely by those who were 15–19 and 25–29 years old.

In 1990 the largest age group is expected to consist of people 30–34 years old. By the year 2000 that group will have aged another 10 years, with the maturation "bulge" represented by people 40–44 years old.[2]

If you're in the business of higher education, these changes will have a great impact, and your program can take advantage of them by developing summer institutes, weekend courses, and education-related travel. For the most part, you'll be looking at informed adults who possess substantial disposable income.

As well-educated parents, these middle-agers will want the best for their children and be willing to invest in programs that provide quality education.[3] On the downside, there will obviously be increasing competition to attract the brightest students—all the more reason to develop an area in which your program is distinctive.

An Aging Society

Baby boomers are not the only ones getting older. Life expectancy for females in 1980 was 77.5 years. In 1990, it will be 79.2 years, and by the turn of the century it's predicted to be over 80. This age will routinely be reached by American women, many of whom will have outlived their husbands by as much as 10 years.[4]

Women who have spent their lives not in the home but in the workplace will on average be living for 15 years beyond what is now the typical age of retirement. The need for orthotic devices, for hearing aids, and for programs which maintain the quality of life in advanced years will become ever more pervasive and compelling.

The number of older persons will also present opportunities for tapping lifetimes of experience. Some of the clients whom you are seeking now might on retirement be willing to work as volunteers in your program. It's not too early to begin shaping programs that will fit their needs and yours.

There will also be a burgeoning need for home health services, nursing homes, and health maintenance programs. Because of the aging population, the opportunities will increase for those skilled in therapy and treatment, including physical and occupational therapists, speech pathologists and audiologists, nurses, and other allied health care providers.

Children Are Being Born with Different Needs

Although it is true that we are aging as a society, it is equally true that we are experiencing a dramatic increase in the number of newborn babies, some of whom survive despite the circumstances in which they were conceived and carried and because of dramatic improvements in neonatal care. As a result, depending on your work setting and location, there may be dramatic changes in the kinds of children whom you will see.

Such changes are due in part to some profoundly sad facts. As reported by the Children's Defense Fund, on any given day

- 2,753 teenagers become pregnant and another 1,287 give birth
- 666 babies are born to women who have not had adequate prenatal care
- 695 low birthweight babies are born
- 1,868 teenagers drop out of high school
- 2,269 children are born out of wedlock
- 36,057 people lose their jobs.[5]

Each of these statistics indicates the difficulty we will have in providing adequate prenatal and natal care. Combined, they are a tragic demonstration of the challenges that will be faced not only by society in general but by all of us in health or education.

Caring for "Preemies"

The good news is that we are learning how to care for children born at risk. The combination of technology and sophisticated intervention techniques that exist in intensive care nurseries (ICNs) across the country are making it possible for babies to survive who are born weighing less than two pounds or carried in the mother's womb for as few as 24 weeks.

But with that improved survival rate comes the potential for numerous other problems. The premature baby may suffer permanent disabling conditions: physical impairment, speech or hearing disorders, or mental retardation. The baby is often, by necessity, removed from prenatal care and from the normal nurturing process, and it may be years before we discover what effect such isolation and the absence of normal nurturing will have on the developing child.

The need to provide both preservice and in-service training to professionals who will work with such children and with their families will mushroom, due in part to the passage of federal legislation mandating that these children receive proper individualized care. So, too, will the need to improve the state of primary prevention, which can be done by anticipating the problems, working with the community, and offering guidance to students and adults before they become parents. In both educational and health settings, the challenges that surround perinatal care offer opportunities for new programs that can dramatically improve the chances for babies to thrive.

We May Become a Nation of Minorities

Historically, the main source of immigrants to this country was Europe. However, during the years 1981–1985, some 48 percent of all legal immigrants came from Asia. Another 35 percent came from Latin America. The number of illegal immigrants in this country grows by some 500,000 a year, three-quarters of them from Latin American countries. At the same time, the native birth rate has slowed, so that immigration accounts for one in four new Americans each year.[6]

Hispanic Americans

By the year 2000, there will be some 26 million Hispanic Americans, most of them originally from Mexico. What does this mean for your program? It could mean some enormous opportunities, especially, but not exclusively, if you are living in the Southwest.

Here are some ideas for programs that might be worthy of your consideration:

- Establish a focused outreach program to help meet the needs of Hispanic immigrants, many of whom will never learn English, even as a second language.
- Create a training program for your institution's professional staff. (What about seeking a grant to develop a cultural awareness program that would be planned and conducted by skilled persons of Hispanic background working in your department?)
- Pursue opportunities for developing or modifying appropriate tests and for working with school systems to devise effective placement strategies.
- Educate local employers who will increasingly need to learn how to recruit, hire, train, supervise, and offer advancement to individuals of Hispanic origin.

Black Americans

The special needs of Black Americans, particularly those in large urban areas, will grow more acute in the next decade. In terms of their economic status, Blacks are increasingly becoming divided into two dramatically different cultures. On the one hand are those who have completed high school or even college and are a part of the mainstream in terms of career, home, and family. On the other hand are those who are able to find only temporary, low-level work—if they find any work at all.[7]

The result is what the Ford Foundation refers to as "the new permanence of poverty,"[8] poverty that is concentrated in center-city ghettoes. Data from two major American cities bear this out. In 1970 about 15 percent of New York City Blacks lived in what were considered high-poverty neighborhoods. In one decade that percentage jumped to 45 percent. In Chicago, the percentage went from 25 to 50 percent in that same period.[9]

Asian Americans

The continuing influx of Asian Americans, who have generally shown a great desire for education, may influence program recruitment efforts. (Rural and remote populations, minority and otherwise, provide unique oppportunities for programming that builds on the possibilities offered by telecommunications and other technologies.)

Health Issues Are Societal Issues

Whether your primary work setting is Colby College in New England or Children's Hospital in Los Angeles, your program will be impacted by several major health issues. Consider what type of program you could develop in response to the following.

AIDS

Whether you work primarily with babies or adults, in special education or nursing, your program, in all likelihood, is going to have to address how to help persons who have contracted the human immunodeficiency virus (HIV), which results in AIDS. It is hardly too soon to begin formulating plans for in-service training and for helping your institution address this issue in a manner that is both compassionate and considerate of those you serve who are not infected with HIV.

Drug Abuse

As with AIDS, the effects of drug abuse are becoming so widespread that if you don't plan how your program will address them, someone may do it for you. It is in your interest to consider how to take a proactive stance by developing a new initiative. How will drug abuse affect the kinds of clients that your center sees over the next ten years? What kind of educational programming might you jointly undertake with the local community? What can you do to further the image that your program is "out in front" on issues such as this?

Not that you need to be out in front, or ought to be, on every issue that arises. The point being made here is that you need to be sure that you have considered issues such as AIDS and drug abuse and know how you will address them.

Wellness

Diet, exercise, wellness, holistic health. Health promotion, disease prevention, stress management, aerobic benefit. Fiber, low salt, Pritikin. Fonda, Sorensen, Cooper.

In case you've missed it, we are in the midst of a wellness revolution, a revolution that presents great opportunities for developing programs within both health and education. It is not difficult to think of wellness programs that could be offered to the relatively affluent parent or to the retired female. Come up with a way of infusing the concept of wellness into the thinking of kids who are likely candidates for drug and alcohol abuse and you would really have something. It's doable, and creating a successful program would surely be worth your effort.

We Are Redefining "Home" and "Family"

Those of us whose family comprises 2 parents, between 2 and 2.3 children, and 1 dog, all living in a detached house, are in the minority, as can be seen from the facts cited below.

Living with One Parent or No Parent

A greater percentage of Americans either live alone or with someone with whom they are not related than at any time in the past 50 years.[10] One in two marriages now ends in divorce.[11] Combine this statistic with the fact that many people do not think it essential to marry in order to have children and one can understand the prediction that as many as 60 percent of children recently born will spend some portion of their childhood with a single parent, most likely the mother.[12]

Smaller Families

As a result of the increase in single parenting and the decrease in the birthrate, the average household size has been reduced. In 1960, families of four or more composed 40 percent of American households. By 1980, that percentage was reduced by 10 percent, and the trend continues.[13]

More Money, Less Time

There is no one home during the day. If there are two parents, both work. As a result, families have appreciably more income to spend and less time to spend it. Health care and elective education will increasingly have to take account of this situation by going into the workplace, by offering clinical hours on weekends and evenings, and by providing services in nontraditional settings.

If your program has not yet begun to address these realities with new "product lines," now is none too soon. Perhaps your facility has the capability to offer local employers a menu of health-related services provided in community settings or even within the workplace itself.

Perhaps you can develop courses that serve the needs of single or working parents. The content of these courses might not be dramatically different from what you now offer, but they would have an added focus on the needs of this emerging market for your services. How about holding an informal focus group with employees of a local company or with parents of a nearby school to ascertain needs and discuss ways in which your own program might fill those needs?

Our Children Are Less Well Educated Than We

More than one journalist has pointed out that the students now in school may be the first generation to graduate less well educated than their parents. Julian Bond, Georgia legislator, recalls his daughter bringing "a note home from public school in Atlanta that said, 'Julia be late too often.' What kind of teacher wrote that note?" Bond asks. "Is he teaching my daughter to read and write?"[14]

David T. Kearns, president of Xerox Corporation, observes that roughly one-third of American companies are having to teach their employees basic skills. In a speech before the Commonwealth Club of California, he enumerated these alarming statistics.

> If current demographic and economic trends continue, American business will have to hire a million new workers a year who can't read, write or count. . . . America's public schools graduate 700,000 functional illiterates every year. And 700,000 more drop out. . . . American students rank near the bottom of the industrial world's nations in math skills, [and] over a third of our public school teachers of science and math are not certified in those subjects.[15]

In many of the helping professions, the caliber of entering students as measured by Scholastic Aptitude Test (SAT) scores continues to decline. Thus, remedial courses have been included in the curriculum in many colleges.

One of the challenges that we will all face, whether our program is geared primarily to the provision of health care or education, arises from the fact that education appears not to be consistently valued to the extent that it was in previous generations. If education truly is not valued as much, we will be attracting students and staff with less education, less ability to read, write, and think clearly, and less commitment to education as an end in itself.

The challenges facing American education present both problems and opportunities. Those who see the opportunities will begin to develop new programs, make linkages with companies, and position themselves at the hub of a community or statewide team addressing the problems.

There Will Be Clear Limits to What We Can Afford

We have long since learned that the philosophy that underpinned the Great Society was fundamentally flawed. We cannot afford to meet every social need, maintain a huge defense budget, control taxes, and still remain financially solvent as a nation. We are now learning that hard decisions have to be made.

One of the limits will be in the funding available for health care. According to Robert Carriere, a senior executive of Arthur Andersen and Company, before 1995 more than 700 hospitals will cease to exist as independent, tax-exempt entities. Although many of them will be located in sparsely populated areas, some will be in more populated areas but will have continued too long to provide services for which they were not adequately reimbursed.[16] The problem of reimbursement is a growing one: In 1987 there were roughly 37 million Americans with no health insurance and another 15 million who were underinsured.[17]

Skilled Specialists versus Multiskilled Practitioners

Limits in funding will mean that not every traditional discipline will find a place in every health setting. Rather, it is likely that some health centers will opt for the multiskilled practitioner who can perform a range of services traditionally provided only by those with accreditation or certification from a national association. What is emerging is a new discipline that combines skills from several traditional ones. For example, there is a push toward the development of a "gerontologist" credential. A service provider with this credential would not have a background and certification in a particular therapy, but would be a generalist.

Those who have more than discipline-specific skills (for example, courses and experience in administration and management or an in-depth understanding of reimbursement) stand a greater chance of surviving and of moving up the career ladder.

Can We Afford to Save Every Child?

We spoke earlier in this chapter about the dramatic improvements being made in the care of premature infants. The downside of this trend is the cost: A premature baby who spends four months in an ICN and other hospital units subsequently may run up a tab of over $300,000—with no assurance that the baby will live, much less thrive. Access to ICN care is contingent not only on whether the hospital has such a unit but on whether the costs can be managed. Some hard questions arise:

> Is it right to continue aggressive treatment for infants who may not have much of a chance at normal life? And who should decide what is an acceptable quality of life? Should such extensive financial and technological resources be devoted to a relatively few patients? . . . Science and technology do not have the power to tell us when life begins. . . . What they have is the power to give us information and evidence which we must reckon with as we try to draw lines between life and death, fetus and person, mother's rights and baby's rights.[18]

Without so naming it, the writer of the above quotation from *Newsweek* has introduced the concept of *triage*. Triage is a system for deciding the priority of treatment based on estimates of who is most likely to survive.

The Cost of Living Longer

There is a pathetic eloquence to the title of a book published in 1987: *Born to Pay: The New Politics of Aging in America*. Its authors point out that the baby boom generation contributes heavily to supporting the generation that has retired. When the baby boomers in turn become the largest generation of older Americans in history, there will be a concomitant decrease in the number of working-age people to support their needs.[19]

Struggling To Keep Pace

We may be creating new problems faster than we are developing programs to address current ones. We are in a reactive mode, striving mightily to deal with the immensity of current problems (for example, drug abuse) and thereby neglecting to create new programs whose benefits might not be realized for another generation. It seems to be in our nature to focus on today's problems to the exclusion of new efforts which could eventually turn things around.

In addition to creating new programs, it will be necessary to convince administrators, potential funders, lawmakers, and those who implement policy of the importance of *quality* of life.

Here's an example. Recall the case of Barney Frank, one of the first recipients of the artificial heart. As a result of the implant, Mr. Frank lived several months longer than he would have otherwise. Yet during that time, his communication with family, friends, and caregivers was limited to what he could write. With all that we know about alternative communication systems, from sign language to sophisticated augmentative devices, Barney Frank could easily have been provided a means to interact and make his ideas and hopes and fears known. The quality of his life in that brief period could have been dramatically improved.

Why wasn't it? Because we have not done an effective job of convincing others (and perhaps ourselves) that extending life without maintaining its quality is of questionable value. With the burgeoning senior citizen population, the opportunities for "selling" this concept are tremendous and should not be overlooked.

Institutions Aren't What They Used To Be

There are numerous indications that the roles of traditional institutions such as those we studied in Sociology 101 are changing and their traditional functions are being provided in nontraditional ways. Here are two examples.

We're All in Business

The line between business and service, between for-profit and nonprofit, is becoming thinner even as you read. It was fashionable a few years ago for nonprofit organizations that considered themselves on the cutting edge to talk of marketing plans. Now marketing plans are essential for their survival. At the same time, the Small Business Administration, and small businesses themselves, are very much threatened by the incursion of non-profits into proift-making ventures.

So what? How's that affect your program? For one thing, if you're not thinking of ways in which you can bring in revenue beyond student or client fees and fund raising, you may be missing some real opportunities. We'll talk more about them in Chapter 12.

The "business" of nonprofits also affects how your program is viewed and how you need to view it. If you are uncomfortable with budgets, with forecasts, with the development of business plans, you're swimming against the tide. It's time to take a course or two.

Business As Caregiver

While those of us in the nonprofit world are becoming more businesslike in the way we think and act and perhaps even dress, businesses are taking up the slack in regard to some human needs: day care, shelter, education, health care, and even moral values. Businesses are on their way to becoming the largest providers of adult education, if they are not that already. As part of the wellness phenomenon, businesses are offering courses in disease prevention and stress management as well as opportunities for employees to obtain confidential drug and alcohol abuse counseling. Inevitably, they will be providing or paying for the provision of day care as well.

All of this can eventually benefit your program. Businesses are increasingly going to look for ways in which they can purchase both health and educational services for employees and their families.

Our Values Are Changing

Your ability to effectively devise and implement plans will be enhanced by understanding the shifting value system in this country.

Authority and Responsibility

There is an overall decline in the respect for authority. Within employment settings this is evidenced by the desire for a more participatory form of decision making. With regard to personal health, people are less inclined to follow the pronouncements of physicians and more desirous of taking charge of their own health (another indication of the wellness phenomenon). In general, authority figures simply do not command the same unquestioned respect and obedience that they used to.

This trend offers some opportunities to involve others—staff, students, or clients—in thinking about what you do well and what new endeavors you might pursue.

Quality and Quantity

There is some evidence of a slowing down in our desire to acquire. *Newsweek* magazine, writing about the changing values of yuppies (young urban professionals), notes that "BMW's and the almighty buck are out."[20] That may be something of an overstatement: BMW dealers are not likely to need our sympathy in the near future. But nonetheless, there is some indication that we are generally looking for more ways to add meaning, instead of accouterments, to our lives.

That's a good thing for any program striving for excellence, as long as the program's attributes are made well known. And it bodes ill for programs not concerned about quality, as well it should.

People versus Institutions

A corollary to the lower value placed on authority is the lower value placed on institutions by young adults, who tend instead to put their trust in people. What does this imply for program planning? First, for certain constituencies your program may need to stress its superior staff rather than the institution's longstanding reputation, whereas older individuals may perceive the reputation as the main attraction. Second, a program housed in an institution with a less-than-outstanding reputation may be little hurt by that reputation. Such a program can build on the characteristics and accomplishments of its own staff, playing down its connection with the institution.

There is a further aspect of this trend to value people over institutions: It is more important than ever to remember that what we are doing makes a difference in the lives of people. We tend to avoid talking about our programs in terms of the benefits they provide to people, fearing that it's "schmaltzy" or that it lessens our professionalism. We will need to become more comfortable in certain venues talking about our work in human terms—not clients but people, not research n's but numbers of people positively affected.

Self versus Group

Tied up with the decline in respect for authority and institutions is a trend toward valuing ourselves and our own fulfillment over the interests of particular groups to which we might belong. That trend can be viewed as at once both selfish and enlightened. As supervisors, we will benefit from being mindful that among younger staff the desire to develop their potential may outweigh the value they place on helping the department to succeed. What we need to work out is a strategy that allows everyone to win.

Daniel Yankelovitch addresses this search for self-fulfillment in his book *New Rules: Searching for Self-Fulfillment in a World Turned Upside Down.* He argues that the search for self, the preoccupation with self, is not necessarily the same as egocentrism. Indeed, it is a journey toward a goal that is as important for society as for the individual. . . .

> The self-fulfillment search is a more complex, fateful, and irreversible phenomenon than simply the by-product of affluence or a shift in the national character toward narcissism. It is nothing less than the search for a new American philosophy of life. . . . It is not that the new philosophy of life rejects materialistic values: Americans are far too practical for that. But it broadens them to embrace a wider spectrum of human experience. Under its influence, Americans may become less self-absorbed and better prepared to face the difficult choices that now confront our civilization.[21]

Yankelovitch argues that our focus on ourselves ("What's good for me? What's in it for me? How will it help my career?") is only one stop on a longer journey, a journey that he thinks will eventually result in a new "ethic of commitment" based on the idea that what's good for "me" will be interrelated with what's good for all. If he is right—and our next section, on volunteerism, supports his view—then this is a trend worth closely watching. More than that, we would all do well to think how we can incorporate it into the mission and philosophy of emerging programs.

Said another way, if we can design our programs so that they allow the pursuit of individual goals of self-actualization (in order to attract top talent) and also contribute to the greater social good (both now and in the future), then we're really onto something. There are only so many good ideas floating around at any one time. If this is one of them, it merits tuning out other distractions for a while in order to ask ourselves how we can develop program concepts that serve the greater good and at the same time the interests of individuals, be they department staff, administration, or donors.

Volunteerism

Across virtually all age categories, both the percentage of people who volunteer and the amount of time volunteered are on the rise. Nearly half of the respondents in a 1988 Gallup poll said that they were volunteers or involved in some kind of charitable work; 37 percent said they were giving more time as volunteers than they had three years previously.[22]

As a measure of their corporate consciousness, companies are becoming favorably disposed toward lending executives to nonprofit organizations. The 1987 annual report of IBM, for example, included a section entitled "Corporate Citizenship: An Ongoing Commitment," which contained the following quotation: "The company sponsors many programs to encourage and support employees in their efforts to benefit their communities and society as a whole."[23]

Taken together, the trends of volunteerism and corporate citizenship are good news for programs seeking financial support, both in dollars and in contributions of time. Indeed the two forms of support go hand in hand. The volunteer who helps out in your clinic is becoming invested in what you do and is thus a natural advocate when it comes to getting backing from others of wealth and influence.

We spoke briefly in the chapter on planning about "reframing," that is, looking at a situation from a different perspective in order to see possible opportunities instead of only problems or threats. So many of the trends discussed in this chapter can be viewed either as problematic or as offering potential. Some of the best programs in the country resulted from confronting a problem that needed to be addressed. It's a matter not of changing the picture but reframing it. It's a matter of discovering new ways in which to respond, ways that will lead to the betterment of society as well as our own programs.

NOTES

1. John Naisbitt, *Megatrends: Ten New Directions Transforming Our Lives* (New York: Warner Books, 1982), 24.

2. *American Demographics* 5 (January 1983):46–47.

3. John Naisbitt, *John Naisbitt's Trend Letter* 7 (January 21, 1988):1.

4. Gregory Spencer and John F. Long, "The New Census Bureau Projections," *American Demographics* 5 (April 1987):27.

5. These statistics are taken from a 1988 advertising flyer for the Children's Defense Fund, Washington, D.C.

6. "U.S. Could Become a Nation of Minorities," *The Futurist*, March-April 1987, 57.

7. Reynolds Farley, "The Growing Gap between Blacks," *American Demographics* 5 (July 1983):17.

8. *The Ford Foundation Letter* 19 (June 1988): 1.

9. Ibid., 2–3.

10. Joseph F. Coates and Jennifer Jarratt, *Future Search: Forces and Factors Shaping Education* (Washington, D.C.: National Education Association, 1987), 13.

11. Ibid.

12. Joseph F. Coates and Jennifer Jarratt, *Studying the Future* (Washington, D.C.: Joseph F. Coates, 1987), 7.

13. Joseph F. Coates and Jennifer Jarratt, *Future Search*, p. 16.

14. Pete Hamill, "Breaking the Silence: A Letter to a Black Friend," *Esquire*, March 1988, 98.

15. David T. Kearns, in a speech delivered to the Commonwealth Club of California, July 10, 1987.

16. Robert Carriere, quoted in "Special Conference Report," *Fund Raising Management* 18 (January 1988):64.

17. Vernon R. Loucks, Jr., speaking before the Health Industry Club, Harvard Business School, October 8, 1987.

18. Barbara Kantrowitz, Pat Wingert, and Mary Hager, "Preemies," *Newsweek*, May 16, 1988, 64.

19. Phillip Longman, *Born to Pay: The New Politics of Aging in America* (Boston: Houghton Mifflin, 1987), 72–74.

20. Annetta Miller, Carolyn Friday, and Sue Hutchinson, "The New Volunteerism: High-Paid Yuppies Are Penciling Compassion into Their Calendars," *Newsweek*, February 8, 1988, 42.

21. Daniel Yankelovitch, *New Rules: Searching for Self-Fulfillment in a World Turned Upside Down* (New York: Random House, 1981), xix.

22. Virginia A Hodgkinson and Murray A. Weitzman. *Giving and Volunteering in the United States: Summary of Findings from a National Survey* (Washington, D.C.: Independent Sector, 1988), 5–6.

23. *IBM 1987 Annual Report* (Armonk, N.Y.: IBM Corporation, 1987), 22.

Five Key Steps in Planning for Your Program

The best way to predict the future is to invent it.

Alan Kay
Apple Computer

In Chapters 2–4 you did three things:

1. You engaged in a visioning exericse, imagining what your program might be like in five years.
2. You noted your strengths and weaknesses and identified the constraints and opportunities that exist within your institution.
3. You looked at possible trends with an eye to how they might affect your program and how you might incorporate them into your planning.

You're ready to nail down a plan, to invent the kind of future that you want your program to have.

Planning for the success of your program involves five sequential steps. They are hinted at in the word *DREAM*:

- Designing
- Refining
- Executing
- Acting
- Modifying

There's nothing magic about the number five. Yet there are enough discrete elements that planning can't be done in much less than that number of steps, and probably if you thought you had to go through ten different steps you would be tempted to say the heck with it.

Obviously, there is some point in choosing *DREAM* to remember the five steps. That is what planning is all about, isn't it? Dreaming and then making the dream real.

DESIGNING

What makes a building unique? What makes one novel stand out in our minds? One movie? Perhaps the answer is that most memorable works of art have a pervasive theme. We may never consciously analyze just what the theme of a work of art is, but its presence is felt.

Designing a Theme

Successful programs do not necessarily do everything well. Indeed, it's almost axiomatic that a jack-of-all-trades is a master of none. This is borne out by the work of Peters and Waterman, whose *In Search of Excellence* discussed what made some companies so successful. They found that the excellent companies were able to keep their focus on a small number of values and objectives. "The focus on a few key values lets everyone know what's important,"[1] making it easier for everyone on the "team" to internalize the values the company has set out.

Peters and Waterman point to the example of Texas Instruments, where the watchword is "more than two objectives is no objectives."[2] The point is that, at least in that company's opinion, a person should be pleased to accomplish two objectives in one year.

Designing a theme, a focus, or a core set of values for your program begins with finding a niche.

Finding a Niche: Two Examples

Steinway pianos were for generations the pianos to buy, because of the quality of their sound, the evenness of character across each note, and their durability and beauty.

Competing with Steinway was like competing with Johnny Carson; one was doomed to pale by comparison.

Then along came Yamaha. Yamaha studied what Steinway did well and looked for where it could make an impact. What Yamaha found was that Steinway put a great deal of emphasis on the quality of the sound of its pianos but not a lot of emphasis on their reliability or conformity. It was here that Yamaha decided to focus its own development and marketing efforts. For example, one ad read simply, "The Yamaha Piano: because its 12,241 precision crafted parts will stand the test of time."[3] Yamaha introduced, with considerable success, an element of quality that was uniquely its own.

The second example, which is drawn from higher education, concerns a program at a major land grant university in the South. The program had a history of being reasonably good but was largely undistinguished at the national level. In terms of the hypothetical models delineated in Chapter 3, it was a Model 2 program. In other words, it could become successful by identifying what it could do well. The alternative was diminution, if not extinction, should finances become tight.

The program's leadership decided to carve out a niche in the area of computer technology, beginning with some modest programs using Logo to teach children. This strategy resulted in some early successes, and these were shared with other organizations, including potential supporters within the corporate community.

Faculty from the program made a point of speaking at conferences that were important to the program's goals. This visibility in turn made it easier to ask for and acquire equipment from the university. In fact, the university asked members of the department to play a considerably larger role in integrating computer technology within the university itself.

Some of what happened to this program was the result of good fortune. But it wouldn't have happened if the program had not decided on and developed a theme.

Establishing a Mission

Developing a theme starts with determining what you want your program to become, that is to say, its mission. Your institution may well have a written mission statement that says something about education or clinical service, research or training. But if it's like most programs, the odds are good that the mission is not very useful. And it must be, in order to establish the parameters within which plans can be developed.

The point here is that whether or not your institution has a working mission statement, you should have one for your department or division. Your mission statement should complement the institution's (assuming one exists), but it relates specifically to the discipline on which your program is based.

Start Big

One way to begin is to use the technique of brainstorming. You might want to attempt the following exercise, either alone or with a small number of colleagues. The exercise is designed to encourage a maximum number of ideas. (Keep in mind that planning for your program may at first need the involvement of only a small number of persons in whom you have trust and confidence.)

Try setting aside an hour—no phone, no interruptions. These four general guidelines might be helpful:

1. The atmosphere should be a positive one. Ideas—any ideas—should be encouraged and welcomed. The underlying message should be this: "We are here to spin out ideas. Here's your chance to dream about what you think the program can and ought to become."
2. Similarly, the initial stage of brainstorming is not the time to abandon ideas because you think they won't work. If you're using this exercise with your staff, be sure they understand this principle and honor it. At this stage, no idea is foolish or impractical or too wild. Every idea is worth hearing.
3. Encourage not only a quantity of ideas but a quantity of related ideas. Does the curriculum suggested by one colleague stimulate an idea about a course that might be developed? How might a comment on the changing populations that are being served lead to ideas on outreach?
4. Once it is clear that the generation of ideas has been exhausted, it's time to move on to some cleaning up. Are there ideas that might be clustered, joined together, or modified to reflect an emerging theme?

You might want to launch the brainstorming session by sharing your vision of what the program can become in five years and encouraging the other participants to use that vision as a point of departure.

The next step—and your own time will dictate whether this can be done immediately following the brainstorming or after an interval—is to rank what you have developed and refined in brainstorming. One technique that works well here is called *forced choices*. As its name implies, forcing choices demands that decisions be made, with one idea being put ahead of another.

Here's an example of how it might work. Suppose your list of ideas includes the following (your own list will hopefully be longer):

- Develop a course on the social needs of the institutionalized elderly.
- Establish an internship program with a local hospital.
- Incorporate a business management and private practice curriculum into the last year of study.
- Develop an individualized study program for part-time students currently working full time.
- Set up a lab that will allow each student access to word processing, spreadsheets, and the school data base.
- Develop an interdisciplinary major in early childhood.
- Become the best of all similar programs in the region.

- Create a specialization in ethnic and multicultural issues.
- Offer a summer institute in how to use technology to treat AIDS patients.
- Become the principal provider of employee instruction to the XYZ Corporation.

In a group of no more than three (the process can even be done singly), those working on the ranking should begin at the top and make forced choices. For example, they would have to decide this question: "Which would you give up—developing a program for the institutionalized elderly or the internship program with a local hospital?" The "winner" of this forced choice is then pitted against the next item and so on until the ranking of ideas is completed.

REFINING

The exercise on brainstorming was intended to provide a setting that encourages dreaming. The exercise on forced choices helps bring order to that dreaming. Making forced choices doesn't so much limit what you do as order when and how you do it. Items that did not stay at the top may still be worth pursuing, but perhaps not now. Forcing choices allows you to sift your dreams through a reality screen to determine those you want most.

Specifying the Mission

Through a logical series of steps, you are beginning to develop a focus for your program. At this point, a mission, an overriding purpose, may start to become clear. You will see a trend—there are certain items that you believe to be more important than others. What you need to do now is state these in one general, broad, but clear statement that both describes what you want to become and captures the imagination of someone reading it.

The statement may focus on serving special populations. It may emphasize the caliber of program that you want to develop. Or it may combine these two ideas. The important thing is to state—in no more than one clear sentence—what you want your program to become.

How does a mission become a theme? Think of your program as a symphony. Some symphonies are bold, dramatic, and forceful; others are pastoral, lighthearted, and elegant. If the composer's mission is to write a pastoral symphony, he or she achieves this by incorporating that motif into each movement. Similarly, if you decide that your program should be known for its academic rigor, then rigor needs to pervade every aspect of your plan. It needs to come through in what you say about yourself to others. More on this when we talk about case statements.

A Compatible Focus

As indicated earlier, there needs to be close agreement between your program's mission and goals and those of your institution (Figure 5-1). Comparing your goals to those of the institution will also provide something of a reality check. Is your mission feasible? Can it be done within the framework of the larger institution?

What if the answer to either of the above questions is no? What if your mission and the institution's don't seem to be compatible? Following are the alternatives:

1. *Adjust your own mission and goals.* Putting yourself deliberately at odds with your institution might get you accused of having suicidal tendencies. What in the mission of your institution can you build on to enhance both your program and the image of the institution itself? Perhaps you can focus first on a goal that does not seem to be incongruous with the overall institutional position but which, when achieved, will open the door to other opportunities.
2. *Consider how firm the mission and goals of the institution seem to be.* Does your institution have a well-defined sense of where it wants to go? If not, perhaps you can play a role in influencing the larger picture. Would it help to talk with some key players within the institution about developing an overall strategic plan? If you work on a committee that has this charge, your opportunities to influence change increase significantly.

Figure 5-1 Intersection of Missions

3. *Revise your plan in order to reach your goals elsewhere.* This may not be as drastic as it first sounds. You may decide to develop a relationship with another organization in order to initiate a discrete project, being sure that when you do so your own institution is cognizant of and comfortable with your having such a relationship. Perhaps you can link up with a clinic that is interested in serving a population you believe to be underserved. Perhaps you can offer that course on the institutional elderly at another college during the summer.

4. *Become a strategic business unit (SBU) of your institution.* In corporate terms, a strategic business unit "has its own mission and objectives . . . planned independently from the other company businesses. An SBU can be a company division, a product line within a division, or sometimes a single product or brand."[4] Establishing an SBU provides a means for a company or institution to focus on a particular subject. It may be a way of bringing together related activities that are scattered throughout the organization, merging them in order to maximize their potential impact. It may be a way of creating a new thrust for the organization.

Nonprofit organizations have SBUs; they just haven't recognized them as such. The Newhouse School of Communication at Syracuse University, the joint effort of Johns Hopkins University and the Maryland Rehabilitation Center in creating the Center for Technology and Human Disability, the Andrus Center at the University of Southern California—all of these are examples of SBUs within the nonprofit sector.

There are numerous possibilities:

- a center on the traumatically brain-injured child
- a unit bringing together all of an organization's research, services, and training related to the neonatal population
- an institute on health care policy
- an interdisciplinary handicapped studies program that links vocational training and placement programs, rehabilitation hospitals and programs of higher education

To be sure, setting out to become an SBU is hardly an overnight project. But then, what good ideas can be realized without substantial effort? If your institution is not keeping pace with the times, if you have some ideas that don't fit nicely into your institution's mission, developing the concept of an SBU may offer some options.

Good planning is in essence sound marketing—discovering what needs exist and doing something about them. And sound marketing is the basis for getting others to buy in.

EXECUTING

How many long-range plans have you seen that worked? That really seemed to help guide the organization for which they were developed? Why does there so often seem to be little correspondence between the stated plan and reality?

The answer lies in the question: Many plans don't work because there is little correspondence between the plan and reality. In some instances, as indicated above, the goals are unrealistic.

Objectives

Another reason that plans fail is that they do not contain well-defined, measurable, doable objectives. Your mission statement should describe who you are and the marketplace in which you seek to function. Your objectives taken together constitute your marketing plan, and consequently they need to be "intentional, organized and strategic."[5]

Intentional

You can't hit the target if you don't have one. When you move from a broad mission or goals statement, you need to make your intentions clear in greater detail. For example,

By 1990 establish a community outreach program for non-English-speaking residents.

In some instances, the objectives may themselves be a means of measuring your goal. Say the overall goal is to "become the most prestigious psychology program in the tri-state area." That goal could have this as an objective:

Increase the caliber of entering students in the school psychology program by 10 percent.

(*Note*: In this example, you would want to indicate how the "caliber" of students would be measured.)

Organized

The objectives need to be prioritized. Some of this will have been accomplished in making forced choices, but it may be necessary to revisit what you've done to determine if the order makes sense. You may want to move an objective up on the list because completing it will put you in a better position to accomplish another objective.

Strategic

There is no point in identifying an objective that is not integral to the process of getting you where you want to go. Taken together, the objectives constitute your strategy. If each of them gets accomplished, you will have succeeded (probably beyond your wildest hopes). If you have developed an objective that seems important but is not clearly related to the goals you have set out, you need to either rethink those goals or drop that objective. That doesn't mean it isn't important. Many of the items that slide to the bottom of your list as a result of forcing choices will still be considered important. It's just that you need to keep your goals in focus and not be sidetracked.

How many objectives should you have? Probably not more than five or so. (Recall that Texas Instruments tries to limit objectives to two.) Certainly if you have many more than five, your plan will become unwieldy. If you have in mind many more, you might consider either combining objectives or deciding which ones you can currently live without.

ACTING

Developing the action plan is really getting down to business. Just as a plan can falter if you never truly articulate measurable objectives, so too can it fail if you do not make clear what will be done and what will be required to realize the objectives.

Allow yourself the same degree of freedom in determining action steps as you did in identifying major goals.

Mind Mapping

One technique you may want to try is mind mapping. As its name implies, mind mapping translates thoughts into something akin to a road map (Figure 5-2). The process involves developing free-form plans on how to implement a particular objective.

Begin mind mapping by placing one objective in the center of a blank page and drawing a circle around it. Now, what are some ways that you might implement that objective? Sketch a line for each way that you think of and, without worrying about syntax, write down at the end of each line a word or phrase that captures your idea (for example, "Funding," "Develop course outline," "Obtain desktop publishing equipment").

Next, fill in the map by adding additional lines to the main arteries. For example, under "Funding" you might put "Contact alumni" or "Develop approach to General Motors" or "Special Event?" Each of these items in

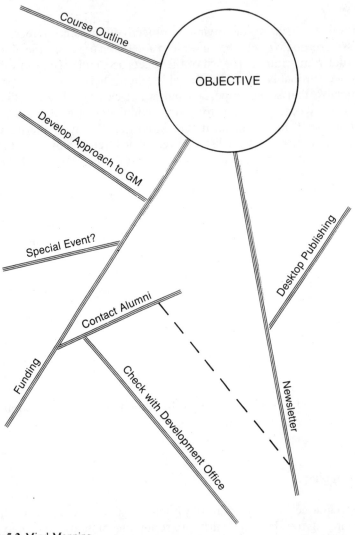

Figure 5-2 Mind Mapping

turn might have a branch or two coming off of it. Under "Contact alumni" you might put "Check with Development Office on Records?" or "Develop mailing list" or "Newsletter."

You may see some ties between various of the lines drawn. If so, connect these by a dotted line.

Once finished with this activity, you should have virtually exhausted the possible action steps for a given objective. Now it's just a matter of selecting the best ones for you and incorporating them into your planning document.

Resources

Take a look at the proposed action steps in order to get an idea of the resources that will be required. You may want to classify the various action steps into the following categories:

1. elements of the plan that can now be started using the resources you have access to
2. elements of the plan that can be accomplished with minimal additional resources
3. elements that will require some kind of commitment from your institution, and perhaps its financial support as well
4. elements that can best be accomplished by obtaining external funding

Scheduling

The timeframe for implementing elements of your plan should be at once realistic and ambitious. Realistic in that you can kill a good plan—and yourself in the process—by trying to get too much done too soon. You need to allow more time than you think will be necessary in order to accommodate new challenges and opportunities.

There's another reason for allowing yourself ample time, which has to do with rewards. If you set unrealistic time frames, you will very soon come to feel that your plan is not working, that your program is never going to get off the ground, and that all your efforts have just been an exercise in futility. Give yourself enough time, however, and you will find you're completing some steps quicker than you had scheduled. Instead of burdening yourself with discouragement, you could then reasonably reward yourself for doing so well.

At the same time, you need to be ambitious in your planning. (It was Andrew Carnegie who reminded us that horse races are often won by the horse that tries a little harder.) Further, your ambitiousness should be reflected in your schedule. If you give yourself six months to write a paper you've been meaning to write, it will probably take six months to finish it. Give yourself two months and you'll find a way of getting it done.

Scheduling Tools

You are likely familiar with at least some of the tools for scheduling activities. No doubt you have used, if not developed, some previously. If you are dominated by left-brainedness, you may relish the development of sophisticated PERT (Program Evaluation Review Technique) charts, in which, for example, Activities 24 and 25 are logical sequelae of Activity

23 and cannot be undertaken until it is completed. There are several effective software packages that allow the use of such "critical path" methods and simplify both their creation and updating.

If you are somewhat less compulsive, a simple Gantt bar chart, which displays the beginning and end dates of tasks, may suffice (Figure 5-3).

What's important is that the tools work for you—and that you don't get so caught up in developing and maintaining them that you lose sight of the goals.

A Word about Detail

As with the development of time charts, the development of the plan should be a means to an end and not the end in itself. It is sometimes tempting to revise, clean up, or expand the plan in order to avoid actually implementing it.

Planning is a process, not a product. It should be a tool that helps keep in focus what you want to accomplish in order to make your program the success that you know it can become. President Eisenhower is supposed to have said that "the urgent things are rarely important, and the important things are rarely urgent." A good plan can help you remember that fact. It can help you keep in mind what is important, recognize that achievements will take time, and not get so caught up in the day-to-day maelstrom that you lose sight of your goals.

MODIFYING

The Washington Redskins won pro football's 1988 Super Bowl with a team that boasted few stars, couldn't make up its mind which quarterback

Month	J	F	M	A	M	J	J	A	S	O	N	D
Hire Project Staff												
Complete Literature Review												
Prepare Quarterly Reports												
Complete Training Manual												
Select Faculty												
Plan/Conduct Teleconference												
Revise Training Manual												
Complete Project												

Figure 5-3 Gantt Bar Chart

to use, lost games that it never should have lost—and then soundly defeated its Super Bowl opponent in a game that was not even close. Why? According to some accounts, it was the team management's ability to adjust, to change their plans not only from week to week but within a game itself, to see new opportunities and to learn from mistakes.

Adapt or Disappear

The health field has its own examples of organizations that learned to adapt their plans in order to survive. One of the best known of these is the Tuberculosis Society, which was created in response to the great number of Americans who suffered and sometimes died from the disease. The Tuberculosis Society might well have gone out of business when TB came under control thanks to early detection and better methods of treatment. Instead, the society turned its focus to other causes of lung damage, most notably environmental ones, and found new life dealing with new causes of harm.

Adjusting to the times is equally responsible for the survival and thriving of occupational therapy, which has come a long way from the limited scope of practice reflected in its name.

The key is the ability to adjust, to see what is coming and turn a possible threat into an opportunity. It's akin to what psychologists call "reframing," altering how we view a situation in order to see what it can offer.

Being able to reframe how you view what's emerging and adjust your plan appropriately is critical to making your plan work. Stagnant plans are just that: inert, stationary, stale. Planning is a circular process, as Figure 5-4 indicates. In planning you constantly have to adjust to take into account what you have learned.

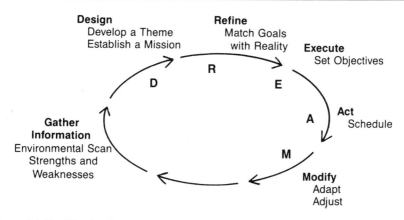

Figure 5-4 The Planning Process

DEVELOPING A CULTURE

Earlier in this chapter reference was made to the book *In Search of Excellence*, in which the authors describe several companies that they found to be unusually successful. A common trait was what Peters and Waterman call "corporate culture":

> Without exception, the dominance and coherence of culture proved to be an essential quality of the excellent companies. Moreover, the stronger the culture and the more it was directed toward the marketplace, the less need was there for policy manuals, organization charts, or detailed procedures and rules. In these companies, people all the way down the line know what they are supposed to do in most situations because the handful of guiding values is crystal clear.[6]

What makes an excellent company can make an excellent program: a shared sense of values, a small number of objectives, a pervasive culture in which the marketplace—the group of people that constitutes the reason for the program—is central. The planning process can go a long way toward creating the foundation for this culture of excellence by investing in co-workers and by giving them the opportunity to help shape programs of vision and devise the strategies by which those visions can become real.

NOTES

1. Thomas J. Peters and Robert H. Waterman, Jr., *In Search of Excellence: Lessons from America's Best-Run Companies* (New York: Harper & Row, 1982), 65–66.

2. Ibid., 75–76.

3. The Yamaha advertisement quoted is the property of Yamaha Music Corporation, USA Piano Division, Buena Vista, Calif., 1987.

4. Philip Kotler and Gary Armstrong, *Marketing: An Introduction* (Englewood Cliffs, N.J.: Prentice-Hall, 1987), 33.

5. James G. Lord, *Philanthropy and Marketing: New Strategies for Fund Raising* (Cleveland: Third Sector Press, 1982), 24.

6. Peters and Waterman, *In Search of Excellence*, 75–76.

Chapter 6

Getting On with It

This is what's called a transitional chapter. You're about to move from planning to implementation. The trick is to determine when the time is right. And you must be wary of the human tendency to procrastinate. As Emerson recommended, "Do not craze yourself with thinking, but go about your business anywhere. Life is not intellectual and critical, but sturdy."[1] If you are inclined to say, with Shakespeare, that "the readiness is all,"[2] remember that it's tempting to say "Not ready" when you mean "Oh, please, not yet."

Planning can, if you're not careful, have a somniferous effect and lull you into complacency. It's tempting to refine, tinker with the language, debate priorities, or rethink methods of implementation.

It's also tempting to focus on reasons, some of them cogent, why this is not the time to start:

"With the staff that I have?"
"The dean would never buy it."
"In this economy, nobody is going to support a new program like the one we've discussed."
"The last thing I'd have a prayer of getting is more staff."
"We just aren't attracting the caliber of students anymore that makes it possible to excel as a program."
"You've got to understand the politics of this place to realize why it's impossible to really get anything done."

Valid reasons. We're all familiar with the expression, "It's hard when you're up to your rear in alligators to recall that your original purpose was to drain the swamp." It is hard but it's necessary. You wouldn't have read this far if you were comfortable with mediocrity.

Henry Viscardi, founder and president of the Human Resources Center on Long Island, had a comment for individuals who pointed out that it was a bad time to raise money or the wrong time for a new school. Viscardi was himself born with stumps for legs and got about on a crude skateboard for the early part of his life, before being fitted with artificial limbs. He developed, in the early 1950s, the first competitive employment program for persons with disabilities. According to Viscardi, "There are always people who will tell you it's not the right time or that conditions aren't right. And for such individuals, it isn't."

And, we might add, it never is.

TAKING YOUR BEST SHOT

So let's take one objective—either one that you think is absolutely essential or one that you think is doable—and get on with it. Set aside time during the day, build it into your schedule, make it as important as anything else you do. Because it is.

ATTRACTING THE NECESSARY RESOURCES

There are only a few ways to secure the resources that you need to begin putting your plan into action:

- You can marry well.
- You can convince your administration that it should provide support.
- You can obtain funding from external sources.

For the sake of argument, we will assume that the first of these is not a reasonable option. (If it were, you probably would not be reading this book.) So the solution is some combination of the other two: getting support from your administration and going after outside funding.

The two are related. In both instances you are seeking to convince someone who does not necessarily share your vision that he or she should invest in you.

GETTING SUPPORT FROM THE ADMINISTRATION

If you incrementally involve decision makers (and those who influence decision making) within your institution, getting support will become a logical next step.

In making your approach, remember the following rules:

1. Illuminate how furthering your program will further the goals not only of the institution but of the people who head it.

2. Ask for an *investment* in what you are proposing, an investment that will have a long-term payoff for the institution.
3. Do your homework, so you know what is likely to "fly." What you want is success. You only hurt your chances for real achievement if you ask for too much (or the wrong thing) and get turned down.

We'll return to the question of how best to work with others within your institution in Chapter 14.

LOOKING BACK, LOOKING AHEAD

We've now completed the section in this workshop in print on planning and are moving on to development, that is, development of the resources that will allow the implementation of your plans.

It's a good time to take stock and remind yourself of the two or three major goals that you have set for your program. Remember when you went to dances as a kid and they stamped the back of your hand? You need to mentally do the same with these goals.

NOTES

1. Ralph Waldo Emerson, from "Essays, Second Series: Experience"; quoted in *The Home Book of American Quotations* (New York: Dodd, Mead & Company, 1967), 408.
2. *Hamlet*, act 5, sc. 2, line 232.

Development: Building for the Future

In the case of fund development, there are no short-cuts to increasing gift support. With few exceptions, increases come as the result of investing resources . . . , good planning and hard work.

Fred A. Matthews and Patricia Lewis
"Long-range Planning in a Short-term Environment"

In the first part of this workshop in print, we discussed planning, which involves understanding trends; understanding your program's strengths, weaknesses, and opportunities; and developing exciting new goals and the plans to achieve them. We considered how best to implement those plans given the realities of your own situation.

We now turn to an essential aspect of implementation, namely, developing the resources that will enable you to achieve those goals without sacrificing existing programs or staff. External financial support, be it from government agencies or private foundations, brings with it an appealing byproduct: the ability to have increased control over what you do and how you do it.

DEVELOPMENT OR FUND RAISING

Although we will use *development*, *fund raising*, and related terms virtually interchangeably, the philosophical underpinnings are clearly those of development. *Development* at one time was paired with *planning* to form the name of many fund-raising offices or departments. The idea is sound: Good development is the product of good planning. As the authors of the epigraph above write,

one reason for long-range planning is that it challenges us to start thinking concretely about the future. An organization needs to start planning how it is to get the resources—human and financial—to make a reality of the vision it has created. This requires a serious assessment of its current situation, the probable costs of the future it has projected and how the bridge to that future will be built.*

As an example, albeit a negative one, the Baltimore Children's Rehabilitation Center (not its real name) some years ago was looking for a director of development and had retained a "head hunter" to search nationally for a suitable candidate. A candidate for the position would have discovered the following set of circumstances:

- The center had a recent history of hiring and firing several directors of development.
- It was seriously in need of external funding if it was to survive.
- There was no long-range plan in place, nor were there any agreed-upon fund-raising goals.
- The center tended to think about its fund raising as it did about its other programs, operating in a panicky "we don't have time to plan" mode.

The center was looking for a director of *development*, but it was thinking *fund raising*.

Development is an integral part of the overall program, driven by proven business practice, informed by planning, and positive in attitude. By contrast, fund raising tends to be isolated ("Let's hire someone to do the fund raising"). It usually operates under limited plans and objectives (if any) and with a crisis mentality.

Whereas development considers the needs and interests of the various populations served by the program, fund raising tries to raise money because "we need your help."

The two also differ in the way they raise funds. Whereas development undertakes research regarding the best prospects and then devises "tailored" approaches to those prospects, fund raising relies on everything from Las Vegas nights to car washes.†

DEVELOPING MARKETS FOR FINANCIAL SUPPORT

Part II considers the various means by which funds can be raised for the betterment of your program. As in the chapters on planning, the ones on

---

* Fred A. Matthews and Patricia Lewis, "Long-range Planning in a Short-term Environment," *Journal of Contemporary Issues in Fund Raising* (National Society of Fund Raising Executives) 13 (Spring 1988): 14.

† For a chart comparing the differences between organized development efforts and not-so-organized fund raising, see Philip Kotler and Karen F. A. Fox, *Strategic Marketing for Educational Institutions* (Englewood Cliffs, N.J.: Prentice-Hall, 1986), 354–355.

development follow basic marketing principles: (1) lay the groundwork, (2) establish goals, (3) do the necessary research, and (4) follow a systematic course.

A WORD ABOUT ATTITUDE

For years we have thought of ourselves as part of the nonprofit world as contrasted with the profit-making sector. We were providers of service, of education, of training. We conducted the research. Our "bottom line" was that we helped people, whereas our counterparts in business had a bottom line measured in income realized.

We have done ourselves and those whom we would help a disservice by clinging to the term *nonprofit* as opposed to *tax exempt*. Tax exempt is a status conferred by the Internal Revenue Service or an equivalent state department of taxation. Nonprofit is a state of mind.

We have not operated with the efficiency of businesses. One result is that some businesses have begun to assume a large chunk of what we once called *nonprofit service*. It is time to take advantage of the fact that we can combine sound business practice with a tax status that allows us to secure contributions. Part II is dedicated to that end.

Chapter 7

Four Steps to Effective Fund Raising

Fund raising is not an event; it is a process.

Edgar D. Powell
Accent on Philanthropy II

Michael Radock, of the Charles Stewart Mott Foundation, argues that 90 percent of the time devoted to seeking gifts should be spent on research, strategy, and cultivation and only 10 percent on the actual solicitation.[1]

Let's take a look at the concepts of research, strategy, cultivation, and solicitation. We will begin with market research and then consider the other elements leading up to the actual solicitation, which will be discussed last.

MARKET RESEARCH

Market research is the process of determining whose interests match yours. In marketing terms, what you want to do is to discover which funding sources within the "universe" of possible sources seem to offer the best opportunities (that is, those who will "buy" the product or service you want to offer). There are some 245 million people in the country and literally thousands of companies and foundations. Broadly speaking, you can segment this universe of potential supporters into three categories:

1. those who are not likely to provide any support (a hospital program in Rochester, Minnesota, is just not likely to appeal to the average citizen in Rochester, New York)
2. those who might support your program generally (for example, "grateful patients" who might make a general contribution if asked)
3. those who might support some particular aspect of your program (for example, a foundation interested in the traumatically brain injured)

The Marketing Process: Two Approaches

The marketing process as it relates to fund raising is not unlike that which would be used in determining the market for any new product, commercial or otherwise.

The process might start from one of two directions, beginning either with needs or with products.

Beginning with Needs

In theory, marketing research begins by determining where there is an unmet need. Let's assume, for example, that we are looking for a business opportunity, a chance to fill a need and make some money. We discern by observation, casual reading, and reflecting on our own experience that there is a need for quality child care. Our next step would be to segment that need: Who needs quality child care and has the wherewithal to pay for it? We construct a demographic profile of those who most need quality day care and are willing and able to pay for it, namely, young, educated, career-minded, two-wage-earner couples (there's probably an acronym there someplace).

What we have found is both a need and a market for our services. Career Day Care, Inc. ("We put the 'care' in 'day care' ") is born.

It is possible to do your own marketing by beginning with needs. In fact, much of the chapter on trends (Chapter 4) encouraged you to consider emerging needs. We suggested several, as well as programs that might be developed in response to them. The same might apply to external funding, but with a caution. In your research you may come across a private foundation that contributes solely to scholarships for students from West Germany. You then have to consider whether seeking such funding is in keeping with your own mission or whether it would be a case of chasing the dollar.

Beginning with Products

While beginning with the needs or desires of the "buyer" is often the preferred approach in commercial marketing, the reverse may be true for fund raising. You have to know what is appropriate for you before trying to match up with a potential source of funding.

The relationship between planning and funding can hardly be overemphasized, as this quotation from professional fund-raising counsel Fisher Howe points up:

> Without a clear statement of mission . . . programs are likely to become confused and useful fund raising impossible. . . .

Do you have clear plans that delineate program priorities? Have you selected certain objectives among the many things the organization might do, and then set goals—measurable achievement points along the path toward each objective? Without such a strategy, fund raising, as well as other elements that contribute to the effectiveness of the organization, will have little meaning.[2]

Programs that have a clear sense of purpose are the most likely to obtain external funding, for several reasons:

- Out of the planning process comes the range of projects that a program desires to undertake.
- Those who have participated in the planning process are familiar with the goals and objectives of the program and are thus attuned to opportunities that might otherwise go unnoticed.
- Funders will want to know what difference their support will make—how it will fit into the larger context. Some may even ask to see the program's long-range plan.

Strategy

Military parlance distinguishes between *strategy* and *tactics*. Strategy is the overall concept, the composite plan of how best to use available resources. Tactics is the actual deployment of those resources.

In some long-range or strategic plans, there is inserted between the mission statement and the delineation of goals and objectives a section called "Strategic Directions." As implied in its name, this section describes the directions in which the organization should be heading. It sets the overall strategy by which the organization will reach its goals, which are directly achieved through the accomplishment of measurable objectives (the civilian equivalent of tactics).

Four Operating Principles

In the case of fund raising, the development of strategies should be done in accordance with the following four principles:

1. Different strokes for different folks. (As we will see in the chapter on private sector support, the approaches used with corporations, individuals, and private foundations differ from each other.)

2. Conversely, there are some common elements of fund raising:
   - Every donor has certain needs and interests, and it is critical to understand what these are.
   - Every donor wants to be thanked.
   - Every donor wants to feel that his or her contribution will make a difference.
   - Donors tend to give in direct proportion to their involvement in the organization.
3. People give to people. Even with the most compelling of causes, the degree of success is increased when the right person does the asking.
4. The various means by which donors might be contacted form a hierarchy. Face-to-face meetings are more effective than the telephone, and the telephone more effective than written correspondence. As for correspondence, a letter beginning "Dear Al" and signed by someone known to Al is more effective than one beginning "Dear Colleague."

How then should you go about developing effective funding strategies? By first determining who are the most likely prospects (the market research) and then tailoring approaches to them. Concentrate first on the best prospects, those not only likely to give but to give substantially. And invest in those prospects the most personalized approaches.

CULTIVATION

Cultivation is an ongoing process that begins with the identification of a good prospect and continues throughout the relationship that may develop. Cultivation is the art of getting a donor to know you, to believe in what you are doing, to feel a part of what you want to accomplish, and to become ever more closely identified with your goals.

In the beginning of the relationship, cultivation of a donor involves some basic information. Say, for example, that you want to obtain support from Mrs. Mildred Maxibucks, a former client or a parent of a former student (either way, she has been identified by your research as being potentially interested in your program).

You may start by inviting Mrs. Maxibucks to an open house, during which you share with a select group of individuals some of the new programs that you are developing. You might have the invitation extended to the group by an "alumnus" of your program (client or student) whose name is well known in the community.

When Mrs. Maxibucks arrives, you personally take her on a tour. Following the event, you send her a handwritten note that states how much you enjoyed meeting her and briefly reiterates some of what you and she discussed.

Over a period of months you correspond from time to time. You send her an article that you wrote. On the basis of her responses, you determine it is time to invite her to join your department's advisory body.

At no point have you asked for her financial support. That will come in time; the cultivation comes first. The better the prospect, the more important the cultivation. Gifts of an endowed chair may take a year or more. But they are worth every moment spent.

And after the first gift does arrive, you continue to build the relationship, going to see Mrs. Maxibucks in her home at her invitation or speaking before a small group that she has organized. You involve her in your planning and indeed develop or modify some plans based on her sound input.

Cultivation. It's a process of education and renewal, of listening and being appreciative. It pays great dividends, not only in dollars but also in the relationships that are established and nurtured.

SOLICITATION

The term *solicitation* is somewhat misleading in that it implies a formal request. Without question, there comes a time in the process when it is appropriate to ask for support. Indeed, the failure of many fund raisers, whether staff or volunteer, is that they find it difficult to move from cultivation to solicitation.

However, if the cultivation has been undertaken with care, the asking will come naturally. There is little need at this point to sell the prospect; he or she is already sold. But the step must be taken, and, as noted earlier, the means by which it is taken will vary according to the potential size of the gift. Making a personal visit to obtain $5 is not a good use of resources. Making a visit to obtain $50,000 obviously is.

NOTES

1. Michael Radock, quoted in *Foundation Giving Watch* (Taft Corporation) 4 (July 1984): 1.

2. Fisher Howe, "What You Need to Know about Fund Raising," *Harvard Business Review* 64 (March-April 1985): 18.

Chapter 8

Obtaining Funding from the Private Sector

Money is not given,
It has to be raised.
Money is not offered,
It has to be asked for.
Money does not come in,
It must be "gone after."

Anonymous

For anyone in the United States interested in obtaining financial support for his or her program, the news is good: Americans are a generous people, and never more so than today. The amount of money contributed to worthy causes continues to rise every year, and this despite the fact that only 25 percent of us are ever directly asked to contribute to a cause and nearly 40 percent of us feel we should be contributing more.[1]

There has been a 257 percent growth in corporate giving in the past ten years.[2] Companies are now matching dollar for dollar the amount of money made available by private foundations. They have become more civic minded out of a sense of "corporate social responsibility," only to be pleasantly surprised to find that there is a direct correlation between philanthropy and business coming in the door. Furthermore, charity promises to continue on the upswing, with groups such as Independent Sector launching nationwide efforts to stimulate volunteerism and encourage individuals, foundations, and companies all to become even more generous.

Nonprofit organizations, some of which were in a panic when the federal funding upon which they had depended began to dry up, are becoming sophisticated in their fund-raising strategies and are applying tools from the business community with excellent results. Consequently, many find themselves more successful than ever before, able to attract new donors and to increase the contributions from existing donors. In short, there is money out there for those who want to go after it intelligently and diligently. And that's what this and the next several chapters are all about.

SOURCES OF FUNDING: THE PRIVATE SECTOR

The following is an overview of potential sources of funds from the private sector, by which is meant all nongovernmental sources of funding, including individuals, incorporated entities such as foundations and corporations, and fund-raising "events."

Working within the System

It is important to note here that if you are in a facility that has a professional fund-raising staff (and it's hard to imagine an institution in health or education today that doesn't), you will be working with and through the "development office" and probably will not be allowed to seek funds directly on your own from private sector sources. Throughout this section are ideas on how to work with your institution's fund raisers. Also, some do's and don't's about working with the development office are presented toward the end of the chapter.

Individual Solicitation

You may already know your best prospects. Why? Because, unless your program has had virtually no record of success, there are people with whom you have come into contact (for example, students, clients, and families) or who know of your program, have been helped by it, and may be in a position now to help you.

Why then don't most program leaders obtain funds from their program's former students or clients? There are probably three reasons:

1. Most commonly, they haven't thought of it.
2. They may have found it just too awkward to consider asking someone whom they know well, someone whom they've helped.
3. They consider it a breach of confidentiality.

Assuming you've read the first reason above, that no longer applies to you. What about the second? "It's embarrassing. I can't do that. I'm seen as the helper, not the one needing help." This is a real hurdle, perhaps the most challenging hurdle in fund raising. You are faced with the problem of not wanting to ask those whom you know, and yet those who know you are certainly your best prospects.

It may be helpful to remind yourself of the way churches and synagogues are funded. If they didn't ask those whom they are helping to help in turn, churches and synagogues wouldn't exist. Places of worship, which by their nature deal with the most personal and precious parts of our lives, have to rely on the generosity of those whom they serve and know intimately.

Why do people contribute to their place of worship? They believe in what it is doing; they feel they have been helped and their lives have been enriched; and they want to make it possible for that place of worship not only to continue its good work but expand. These are really not so different from the reasons people ought to support your program, which is why you should not hesitate to ask. By asking you are providing them with an opportunity to express their appreciation and to be a continuing part of your effort.

Identifying Prospects

You may well have some prospects for funding currently involved in your program. How do you find out without breaching confidentiality? That's really not so difficult. If you were to ask staff members in your department or division each to make a list of people whom they think might be good prospects, without divulging income, you would find that certain names recur time and again. You will miss some who are not obvious prospects, but if you establish an attitude that encourages those whom you've helped to help you, the odds of your missing out on prospects will diminish dramatically.

"Prospecting," as it is known among fund raisers, can and should also be applied to persons whom you have not helped but who are in a position to help you if they become so moved.

Here is a set of steps you might follow in developing a fund-raising approach geared toward individuals:

1. Determine your organization's policy regarding solicitation of individuals. Do all such contacts require the clearance of the development office?

   Let's assume that the answer is yes, any contact must be cleared through the development office. Keep in mind that the development staff are less interested in seeing a program succeed than in raising money generally—that's the nature of their job. And they won't keep that job for long if they allow you to contact Leonard Lotsabucks for $500 when the president might have been able to get $10,000.

   If you can create a win-win situation, so much the better. In return for your identifying prospects for fund raising, perhaps you can strike a deal whereby
   - you retain some control over the projects for which funds will be sought from these sources
   - you are free to solicit those not considered major prospects, say, those expected to contribute less than $250 annually
   - you receive an "in-kind" benefit, such as the help of the development office in securing a major foundation grant, even when the funds don't go directly to your program.

You have a commodity that development officers want—badly. You have access to many individuals who could contribute large amounts to your organization. In turn, the development office has the knowledge and resources that make for effective fund raising. Many fund raisers feel stymied. They know that alumni, former clients, and friends of the organization are often excellent prospects, but they don't have a way of getting to know these prospects and are sometimes rejected by program directors whom they approach for leads. You can turn that situation around by proposing a team effort that benefits everyone.

2. Inform your staff of your plan, stressing the benefits which can accrue from their participation. Ask each to come up with a list of at least 15–20 prospects.

3. Try to rank the names received on the basis of who appears likely to offer a sizable gift.

4. Coordinate with the development office. Who is the best person to make the approach? Should it be done in tandem?

5. Stay on top of the situation. Don't just turn the matter over to the development staff. These are *your* prospects: Be sure they are not forgotten. In fact, be sure they are well looked after. The development office may send out formal acknowledgments of gifts, which you can follow up with handwritten notes of your own.

6. Say thanks—to your staff, to the development staff who help out, and most especially to those who contribute. Someone who gives once is even more likely to give again, and the person who gave $100 last year is a prospect for $250 this year.

Reasons for Giving

The reasons why people contribute to a cause seem to be changing. Conventional wisdom held that people gave to charity out of guilt, the "there but for the grace of God go I" syndrome. A related motive was the belief that by contributing to a cause one was less likely to be afflicted by the associated harm.

Loyalty to a cause was also presumed to be an important factor, loyalty enjoyed, for example, by religious and educational organizations that could count on support from their constituencies year after year. Grandfather, father, and son all went to Yale, supporting it with their gifts, as well as their presence, generation after generation.

A recent study found that belief in the supported cause continued to be important, but loyalty and guilt were replaced by different factors: (1) belief in the financial integrity of the organization and (2) confidence in the person or persons in charge.[3]

Developing a Strategy

In order to build a successful fund-raising effort, you may want to construct a strategy that takes into account the changing face of giving. Here are five things you might try in cooperation with the fund development office of your institution:

1. State what you do in terms of some "cause." Givers continue to give to something they believe in, something they care about. People want to give not just because it's their school but because that school is making a difference in other people's lives and in the well-being of the country. Your case statement ought to clearly present a cause worth caring about.
2. People tend to give more when asked to pledge. Go for multiyear commitments and don't hesitate to ask someone who has given you $50 to up it to $100.
3. Be sure you present a picture of financial integrity. This doesn't mean you have to look financially secure so much as you have to seem capable of using funding well and committed to using it honestly.
4. Leadership is essential. People bet on other people. If the head of your organization can be an asset to your fund raising, you need to develop ways to involve her or him. If he or she is not an asset, then the need increases for you to become a visible leader. (More on this later.)
5. Spendable, contributable income is highest among those 50–60 years of age, and that age cohort is growing. Target it in your fund-raising efforts.

Asking for Money

You have to be comfortable with the approach that you use to obtain support for your program from individuals. Clearly it is more difficult to ask a person for money than to ask a foundation or a government agency.

Nevertheless, keep in mind that the more personal the approach, the greater the likelihood of getting not only a yes but a bigger yes. It is almost axiomatic that you will not be able to secure a large gift from an individual without cultivating that person one on one.

In descending order, the most effective ways to present your case and ask for support are

1. face to face, with one donor and one solicitor
2. in person, but meeting in a small group (whether the group comprises primarily donors or those representing the cause)

3. by telephone (for example, college alumni solicitation)
4. by personal letter, preferably handwritten
5. by more generalized letter
6. through printed matter (for example, printed letters used in mass appeals by national charitable organizations).

Getting Others To Do the Asking

OK, you begrudgingly recognize that personal contact is going to be essential, especially if you are going to obtain sizable gifts for your program. And, yes, you are willing to make some of those personal visits. But you also have a program to run and have no interest in becoming a full-time fund raiser.

Consider putting a team in place:

- The development office may well be able to handle some of the more routine contribution requests by mail. (But that shouldn't result in your seeing nothing of what comes in.)
- There may be people on your own staff who have the temperament and communication skills necessary to effectively present your case.
- Those whom your program has helped are natural spokespersons, needing only to be asked and coached on what to present. In fact, such individuals are also very good sources of potential prospects. You might consider putting together an informal "alumni council" (*alumni* meaning either former students or clients) that you could turn to for feedback and also for help in your fund-raising efforts.

The potential of involving others who believe in your cause as volunteer fund-raisers is enormous. Some of the largest charitable organizations (for example, United Cerebral Palsy) were started by parents who wanted to see strides made in conquering the disability that afflicted their sons and daughters.

Smaller Givers

The fact that you have identified those who could easily contribute large gifts should not preclude your asking others with whom your program has come into contact. But the greatest amount of effort should be expended on those who have the most potential for substantial contributions. Whereas you should be seeing your very best prospects personally (in their own home if possible), you may rely on a generalized letter to those who are not likely to contribute more than $10 to $25.

Special Events

Special event is a term that refers to any type of fund-raising event, from a bake sale to a black tie dinner. As a general rule, don't put them on:

- They can be very risky. You are at the mercy of competition with other events, bad weather, and the gremlins that love live events.
- You may invest more to put on the event than you raise in ticket sales. Some years ago a two-day rock concert on Long Island brought together the very best rock music talent available and attracted thousands of young people. Unfortunately, it needed tens of thousands of ticket buyers in order to break even.
- You have better ways of using your time. Special events are very labor intensive, sometimes requiring hundreds of volunteer or staff hours. By comparison, one well-researched foundation proposal can raise as much money and only requires a tenth of the time.
- When a special event fails, there is nowhere to hide. If you don't succeed with a written proposal, who knows? If your special event bombs, who doesn't?
- Worst of all, you might succeed, putting your program in direct competition with the institution's own fund-raising efforts.

Suppose, God forbid, that you decide after reading the above to undertake a special event:

1. Select an event with a good benefit:effort ratio. If possible, the event should cost little up front and involve minimal effort on your part. For example, you might link up with a firm that conducts fund-raising special events such as art auctions, where your sole job would be to send out invitations.
2. Consider how you can minimize the time and effort involved. For example, can you recruit volunteers to help? Are there special-event companies in your area that will run an event for you, where you supply the audience and they handle all of the logistics?
3. Maximize the value of the event. Use it to get others to know about your program through handouts, publicity, or an onsite booth. Provide a guest register and write to all who attend, telling them about what you do and inviting their further participation.

Foundations

Grantmaking foundations (known to the IRS as *private foundations*) are at once the most over- and undervalued sources of funding. They are overvalued with respect to their relative importance: Although they provided some $6.3 billion in grants in 1987,[4] that pales by comparison with the $75 billion contributed by individuals. They are undervalued in that they provide a resource that often tends to be overlooked. Ask someone in your institution if they have ever submitted a proposal to a federal agency; the odds are they probably have. Have they ever submitted a proposal to a private foundation? Probably not.

When we think of foundations, we tend to think of the "biggies": Ford, Rockefeller, Robert Wood Johnson. We overlook the considerably smaller ones that are in our own state or community.

The differences between the few truly large foundations and the vast number of small ones are significant:

- Large foundations tend to have professional staff who can be contacted at least by telephone and who review proposals and can help shape them. Most foundations, being small, have virtually no staff and are thus less accessible.
- Large foundations usually have a clear statement of purpose. Small ones typically have interests that are less well defined, and their giving pattern is more a reflection of the personal interests of board members than of definite goals.
- Large foundations tend to support projects that have a national impact or importance; Small foundations tend not to fund outside a prescribed geographical area.[5]

Foundations of each kind have their place and should be researched for possible support. If you can demonstrate that your project has national significance, you may be able to capture the attention of a large foundation. It is certainly worth the investment of your time to look into it. There are major Foundation Center libraries in New York City, Washington, D.C., Cleveland, and San Francisco, and there are cooperating collections in every state. (For information on the whereabouts of cooperating collections, call the Foundation Center toll-free at 800-424-9836.)

Especially with larger foundations, it is possible to obtain a great deal of information: purpose, names of staff and board members (and where they went to school, what clubs they belong to, and so on), a record of grants made, press clippings on recipients or on the foundation, and total assets (and even where the foundation invests its assets).

Segmenting the Foundation Market

For the serious student of foundation research, there are commercial firms that provide periodic information on foundations as well as annual compilations. Of somewhat more use are the computer printouts which can be purchased from the Foundation Center. These are organized by broad categories (Communications, Cultural Activities, Population Groups, Science and Technology, Social Sciences, Welfare, and Other) and then by subcategories. For example, the category Population Groups includes Boys, Blacks, Hispanics, Blind and Visually Impaired, and Deaf and Hearing Impaired.

Comsearches, as they are known, are also available by geographic area, including major cities and certain states and regions. They are also available according to topics within health care (including Cost Containment, Nursing Care, Hospices, Children and Youth, and others) and education (including Adult and Continuing Ed, Faculty and Professorships, Teacher Training, Educational Research, and others).

By combining the data contained in several different comsearches, it is possible to narrow the focus to a foundation that has supported programs like yours and perhaps is even in your area. For example, by drawing on the available searches in three different categories you could begin to determine which foundations might be interested in the idea of a conference on serving a minority population within a rural setting.

- From the category Population you might want a search of the subcategory Hispanics.
- From Welfare you would probably want a search of the subcategory Rural Development.
- Finally, from the category Other you would want a search of Conferences and Seminars to find out which foundations have funded conferences in the past.

One way of undertaking the first level of foundation funding research is to set up a matrix in which projects or your program's areas of concentration are listed horizontally, and potential funding sources are listed vertically. In the example given below (Table 8-1), a sample matrix has been constructed for a program in physical therapy that has an interest in providing services to older persons in outreach settings. The program is currently affiliated with a nonprofit hospital.

The chances are good that your institution, especially if it is a college or university, is tied into one of the electronic data bases, such as the Sponsored Programs Information Network (SPIN) or Dialog, that allow the user to undertake customized searches of funding sources. (A more detailed discussion of both SPIN and Dialog can be found in the next chapter, which is on getting funding from the public sector.)

Smaller foundations, which make up the vast majority, also merit a closer look, although that is sometimes difficult. Although they are required by law to file a 990 tax return, it may be so brief as to offer very little information. The situation is clearly improving, however, and even many small foundations now not only provide information on their funding pat-

Table 8-1 Matrix: Fund-Raising Research

FUNDING DESCRIPTORS

FOUNDATION	Hospital	Health	Gerontology	Community	Handicapped
Fairweather	X				
Heavymetal					X
Ford					
Rockefeller		X			

terns but also retain at least part-time staff who can help you decide whether or not to submit a proposal to them.

A growing phenomenon is the community foundation, which comprises what might otherwise be several very small foundations. By its nature a community foundation tends to have broad and diverse interests that reflect the interests of the people whose funds it administers. The good news is that both small foundations and community foundations are committed to the local community, offering a source of support to programs of quality that cannot demonstrate national importance.

Making the First Approach

Let's assume that you have identified a local foundation that seems to support the kinds of activities involved in your best project. Where do you start?

1. You start with your organization's development office to be sure that you won't be walking into a political buzzsaw if you make contact with the foundation.
2. If at all possible, get yourself properly introduced to someone inside the foundation by someone outside whose name is known and respected. That may take some time. You may want to canvass your own network of contacts (perhaps a staff member of the development office knows someone on the foundation staff).
3. If no such "in" is forthcoming, by all means at least call (after clearing the call with the development office), introduce yourself, and explain briefly what it is you have in mind.

   Let the foundation staff member you speak with suggest the next step, but, if necessary, indicate you would welcome the chance to review your project ideas in person before submitting them formally.

Approaching a foundation requires a great deal of sensitivity. Imagine yourself getting a call each night from someone or other wanting to sell you insurance—just about the time you are sitting down to dinner. You deflect the insurance call only to get another one from say, the Policemen's Benevolent Work Stoppage Society, which is followed by a call from your favorite alma mater or a local charity that has done some very good work with children with mutiple handicaps, and so on.

This scenario is not unlike what foundation staff face. They get calls from causes they would like to see supported and calls they would like to end quickly by just hanging up. Unlike you, they are in the business of giving away money. But having some sensitivity regarding their situation will be beneficial to you. If the staff member you talk to discourages a personal visit, at least you have made your name known and your proposal will remind the staff of your call (all the more reason to be sure the call is a positive one).

Be sure to ask for grant guidelines and an indication of areas of interest.

4. Submit your very best in the form of a concept paper (if that is what is requested) or a full proposal.
5. Follow up, politely but consistently.

Getting to know foundations, and getting them to know you, is not unlike the process of cultivating major individual donors. It takes time to find out their interests and to make them understand the importance of what you do. But it can be well worth the time spent. Foundations are not bound by the strictures that apply to federal granting agencies, which typically require that you apply only when there is an appropriate grant competition. With private foundations, you can submit unsolicited proposals. In fact, that is the fundamental way in which most private foundations operate.

Another benefit in working with private foundations is that the response to your request for support is not always a simple yes or no. The Kellogg Foundation, for example, often works closely with applicants who come in with good ideas, helping them to further shape those ideas into proposals that are compatible with the interests of all parties concerned.

Corporate Support

Corporate giving ranges from supporting the local Little League and purchasing Girl Scout cookies to bestowing some of the most substantial gifts made (for example, a five-year gift from PPG Corporation of $120 million).

Although corporate giving historically has focused heavily on education, specifically higher education, there is some indication that companies are beginning to develop their own corporate-giving philosophies after careful examination of where the needs lie. If this apparent trend holds true, we can expect to see increased corporate giving in response to hunger and other basic human needs; increased support of minority causes, especially those involving Hispanics; and support of programs in behalf of the illiterate, the elderly, and those with AIDS, Alzheimer's, and traumatic brain injury.

In short, companies are becoming barometers of society, with giving patterns that reflect their recognition of the role that they can and probably must play. Ultimately, it is in their interest to provide support to worthy causes.

Getting Support

Officers in charge of corporate giving are popular members of their communities, especially where the company has a policy, as most companies do, of supporting local nonprofit organizations. With all the competition for their attention, how can you get local companies interested in your program?

A hospital outside Washington, D.C., used two methods successfully. One was to secure from the county office of economic development the lists of local employers. This provided the hospital with the names of people to contact. The second method was simple. (It is so obvious and so simple that it is often overlooked.) The hospital served corporate executives and their families, executives from companies such as IBM, Martin Marietta, and General Electric. Corporate funding was easily obtained by identifying the company executives who were patients and then contacting them to ask for their help.

What can you do to secure corporate support?

1. Look at the list of people whom your program has served in the last two years. Whom have you helped who might help you? Is there someone who might be willing to invite his or her corporate colleagues to see your program? Or to send a letter to other corporate executives inviting their financial support?

2. Identify key corporate executives whom you might invite to become involved with you, perhaps serving on a planning task force.
3. What kinds of programs might you offer to local companies, either for fee or as a means of getting them to know you better?
   • A psychology department might do well to offer a course on how to deal with corporate stress.

- A physical therapy department could sponsor a seminar on exercises to avoid lower back pain.
- A hearing and speech department might develop recommended guidelines for industrial hearing conservation.
- A computer science department might develop a team-taught course with the local computer company.

The possibilities are endless. It's really a matter of asking yourself what you know that others need to know or what services you could provide that would benefit a company (and your program as well).

The Nature of Corporate Support

Corporate support can come in the form of cash, equipment, people, and technical assistance.

Cash Contributions. Cash contributions (that is, corporate grants) still represent the most typical way in which companies provide support. Many prefer to give where they have a presence, such as a branch office or subsidiary. For example, the Gannett Company, publisher of *USA Today,* will only contribute to locales where it has plants. That makes the job of getting support both easier and more difficult. It means a program may be ineligible for support from a company like Gannett if it is not located in the area, but, on the other hand, the program can more easily capture the attention of companies who are in its area.

Cash contributions may also result from what is called *cause-related marketing.* American Express Company was one of the pioneers of this approach. Here's how it works. American Express and Upscale Department Store might agree to combine forces in order to support the community's historic preservation effort. For thirty days, a percentage of all Upscale sales charged to American Express go to the historic preservation society. American Express gets an increase in use of its card, Upscale enjoys greater sales, and the historic preservation society gets a contribution for which it had to do very little.

Contributions of Equipment. Contributions of equipment are rapidly coming to rival cash contributions. Giving away equipment is easy for a company to do; it allows writing off equipment that may have already been depreciated or that exists in overabundance in the company's inventory, and it can be used to "seed" the market. Apple Computer, for example, contributes blocks of new equipment in order to establish a presence in a desired market.

How do you find out about the availability of gifts of equipment from companies?

First, by getting the companies in your area to know you, so that when equipment becomes available they think of you.

Second, through research. As with foundations, there are published directories of corporate grants, including grants of equipment.

Third, by utilizing mediator or broker organizations established for the purpose of linking companies giving away equipment with nonprofit organizations. One of these broker organizations is the National Association for the Exchange of Industrial Resources (NAEIR). NAEIR is a nonprofit association that contacts businesses not only to learn the whereabouts of excess or slow-moving inventory but also to collect that inventory. NAEIR then makes its information available to its members. Four times a year NAEIR publishes gift catalogs from which member organizations can order free equipment, paying only shipping and handling costs. Items include everything from art supplies to computer equipment. Membership in NAEIR is open to any nonprofit, tax-exempt U.S. organization. For information contact NAEIR at 560 McClure Street, Department NP-1, P.O. Box 8076, Galesburg, IL 61402.[6]

Another equipment broker is Gifts in Kind, which is the United Way's distributor of corporate in-kind contributions. It specializes in "high tech," specifically hardware and software, and among the companies who have used Gifts in Kind to distribute equipment are 3M, Digital Equipment Corporation, Apple Computer, OKIDATA, and Motorola Corporation. One need not be a United Way agency in order to participate. For further information, contact your local United Way and ask for the Gifts-in-Kind coordinator.

Contributions of Human Resources. One of the most valuable corporate contributions is the making available of human resources in the form of "loaned executives." When this concept first appeared, it was met with skepticism. Some nonprofits looked askance at the offer, wondering why a company would loan out a high-paid, talented executive to a nonprofit organization. Surely, such a company would only use this scheme to unload the unwanted. And corporate executives understandably asked, What happens to my career during the year or two that I'm on leave?

Truth be known, the loaned executive program may have provided companies with a means to ease certain employees out. That criticism is not valid today, however. Coincident with the growth in corporate social awareness has been the willingness of some very talented people to step off their career paths for a time in order to be of service to others. When Howard University wanted to set up a computerized management information system, it was able to convince IBM to provide it with loaned talent. The same has been true for schools of engineering and science.

How does one go about getting a loaned executive?

- Articulate a clear need that can best be met by someone from the corporate sector.
- Develop a specific time frame in which that person will be engaged (open-endedness suggests you haven't thought the project through well enough).
- If you know someone within the company from which you'd like a loaned executive, start there. Ask him or her to find out the official and unofficial rules that apply. For example, would it be best to address your request to the manager of the local branch or are such decisions only made at corporate headquarters?
- Find out the extent to which the company has loaned executives in the past. If your request can model a request that was approved, your chances increase of getting a yes.
- Consider who should make the request. Would it be more compelling if it came from someone higher up in the administration? Can the development office be of any help?

Indications are that the loaned executive concept is burgeoning. Companies that have not previously loaned out staff are beginning to do so, and some companies with a history of loaning are expanding their programs. This is due in part to the swelling presence of baby boomers in managerial positions. In order for them to move up career ladders, companies need to make space available, and loaning executives is one way of doing this.

The benefits of being loaned a corporate executive can go well beyond the fact that you temporarily have an additional staff member. Among other things, the loaned executive is a potential advocate. If he or she comes to believe in what you are trying to accomplish, it could lead to donations of equipment, corporate grants, and even help in soliciting other companies for support. Hence the importance of developing a project that the executive will feel good about and of ensuring that the working climate is a positive one.

An alternative to being loaned an executive is being loaned technical support. You may not need a full-time person on staff but could benefit from access to expertise, for example, in marketing your program, developing printed materials, or even developing a training program that you can turn around and offer to the company doing the loaning.

The Bottom Line

Although it is true that companies contribute outside of their own areas of interest (Exxon's support of the arts is a prime example), it is also true that a company is going to be more inclined to become involved if it can see a benefit for itself. All things being equal, if your program can offer something that fits the mission and objectives of the company, you stand a better chance of garnering real support.

No organization understood this better than the Children's Museum in Denver. At one time the museum was in such serious financial difficulties that it was uncertain whether or not the payroll could be met. The museum's board brought in a new executive director with a business orientation. He asked his staff and himself who might want or need what the museum could provide, namely, access to children and their families. The answer: companies with products to sell.

Within months, he had a contract with MacDonalds to produce a coloring book based on exhibit material within the museum and another with a major airline that was looking for in-flight material that would be of interest to parents flying with young children. Within two years, the museum was not only financially solid but was raising the majority of its budget through corporate support. The reason is clear: The museum had developed a marketing plan that took into account the needs and interests of donors, in this case, corporate donors.

One caution: Keep focused on the kinds of programs that fit your mission and the mission of your institution. It can be very tempting to overstretch in order to accept outside funding.

WHERE TO START

Individuals, corporations, private foundations, special events. How does one decide where to start?

The answer lies in two basic principles of marketing and planning that have been referred to throughout the book thus far:

1. Determine your best prospects. Marketing starts with an analysis of the marketplace. Does your program have a large pool of potential individual donors? If so, you may want to start there. Are there many companies in the area? If so, what is their economic condition? Are there private foundations within the community or state?
2. Consider where your strengths lie. Do you have the kind of program that might appeal to the corporate sector? Do you view yourself as having strong interpersonal skills? How well would you do in a one-on-one meeting with a potential major donor?

Analyze the market. Analyze your strengths and weaknesses. And then go for it. Don't put off fund raising until some magic set of circumstances occurs. Make it a component of your program. If you have three goals, make fund raising one of them.

NOTES

1. Richard Wilson, "Megatrends in Fund Raising," paper presented at the American Society of Association Executives Fifth Annual Management Conference, Nashville, Tennessee, November 1987.

2. "Key Fund Raising Statistics," *Fund Raising Management* 18 (November 1987): 32.

3. Wilson, "Megatrends in Fund Raising."

4. "Key Fund Raising Statistics," 32.

5. *Foundations Today: Current Facts and Figures on Private Foundations,* 4th ed. (New York: The Foundation Center, 1986), 6–7.

6. *Health Funds Development Letter* (Health Resources Publishing), December 1986, 2.

Chapter 9

Getting Uncle Sam To Support Your Program

The phrase "Federal financial assistance" includes any form of loan, grant, guaranty, insurance payment, rebate, subsidy, disaster assistance loan or grant, or any other form of direct or indirect Federal assistance.

Application for Federal Assistance

Getting financial support from the federal government is as different from getting corporate support as Washington, D.C., is from Chicago. We will focus on the federal government in this discussion of public sector support for two reasons:

1. State and local governments vary widely as regards the types of programs they will support, and the reader would do best to access specific information directly.
2. The type of proposal that needs to be developed for state or local support bears a similarity to the type for federal agencies, and preparation of such a proposal is addressed in Chapter 10, "Characteristics of a Good Proposal."

TYPES OF SUPPORT

Although there is a range of possibilities for federal support, the most common types are grants and contracts.

Grants

Grants are more common than contracts as sources of financial support for nonprofit organizations. Grant proposals can be developed and submitted "unsolicited" to a funding agency. The unsolicited approach is favored by research agencies within the National Institutes of Health (NIH). The proposal format remains standard, and anyone can develop and submit a proposal at virtually any time to the institute that most fits the proposal's content.

The more usual strategy is to respond to an agency's grant announcement. An agency utilizes a grant announcement to inform interested parties that the agency is encouraging proposals that address a certain topic area. Often such areas have been prescribed by law (for example, the recent emphasis on children aged 0–2). A description of the exact format that must be followed in order to submit an acceptable proposal in response to a grant announcement will be contained within the application "kit" that accompanies the announcement, as will a description of the means by which proposals will be evaluated.

A variation on the grant announcement is *field-initiated research,* where an agency encourages submission of proposals without determining priority areas for applications. Field-initiated research is similar to the approach used by NIH, in that the applicant is free to determine the area that will be studied; however, it is dissimilar in that there is not an open time frame within which to submit a proposal. If you miss an NIH deadline, another will occur in four months. If you miss the deadline for a field-initiated research competition, you're out of luck. Grant proposals are usually reviewed by a panel of experts in the field (a panel typically is composed of three people). They read the proposals independently and then usually meet in order to make their recommendations to the agency as to which proposals merit funding according to the prescribed criteria. For any competition, the agency may have several panels reading proposals. It is then up to the agency to group the scores from the various panels and select those organizations that will be funded.

Contracts

A contract is just that: a legally binding agreement between you and the federal (or state or local) agency. The agency says, in effect, we want this work done, in this period of time, according to these conditions. For example, Head Start may decide it wants a study conducted to determine if Hispanic children are benefiting from Head Start as much as African American children. It specifies the information it wants gathered, from whom, and over what timespan. It may describe precisely the means by which the information is to be gathered (for example, telephone or mail survey, field site visits) and how the information is to be analyzed and reported. The agency indicates by person-years or -hours how large it believes the job will be (one person-year is roughly calculated to be $75,000). For example, the agency may estimate that the proposed "scope of work," as it is known, is five person-years. Those interested in bidding on this contract thus know that in order to be competitive, their proposal needs to cost out at about $375,000 (or less). Naturally, if they can submit a sound proposal with a smaller amount, their chances of being awarded the contract increase.

The funding agency may invite certain firms or organizations to bid on a request for proposal (RFP), or it may publish an RFP as an open competition. Unlike grant proposals, contract proposals are typically reviewed by agency staff, sometimes bringing in experts from another agency. Contract proposals are submitted in two parts: (1) a technical proposal, which details how the bidder is going to accomplish the work and his or her capabilities to do so, and (2) a business proposal, which details the costs involved. The two proposal elements are reviewed separately, with the intent of selecting as the winner the bidder who offers the best combination of technical capability and price.

Grant or Contract: A Comparison

When most of us think of obtaining federal financial support, it is grant support that we have in mind. Grants allow programs to conduct research in their areas of interest, to provide preservice or in-service training, to establish demonstration projects, or to develop new curricula. By their nature, grants provide recipients with greater latitude. It is the recipients who determine what projects they want to work on and who then develop proposals to obtain funding. Agencies generally are more tolerant of changes in the scope of work for grant-funded projects, allowing recipients to make some modifications and stretch out the timelines somewhat.

There are certain drawbacks to grant funds that you need to be cognizant of. One is that the amount of money available per average grant award tends to be less than that for the average contract.

Also, grant award competitions often specify the amount of overhead that can be charged. For example, training grants may allow the recipient to recoup only 8 percent of direct costs. (Hence, if the total direct costs come to $75,000, the recipient can charge no more than $6,000 to recoup all associated indirect costs, such as for building occupancy, heat and light, administrative services, and so on.)

By contrast, contracts generally allow the recipient to charge not only full indirect costs but also, where applicable, a fee for profit. (Hence, if the total direct contract costs were $75,000, and the recipient figured the indirect costs at 65 percent of personnel costs, the recipient might well charge some $14,000 in indirect costs, assuming the personnel costs were about one-third of the total budget.)

Why Not Go Mainly for Contracts?

So why wouldn't it make sense to concentrate on contracts, where the dollars are bigger and the payoff greater? For consulting companies, it does make sense.

Much of the contractual work of the federal government—and not only of the Department of Defense—is conducted by companies whose business is largely derived from government contracts. However, although these companies sometimes specialize in certain areas (for example, education policy or survey design), they operate in a responsive mode. That is, they very closely monitor all sources of government funding information and regularly bid on contract RFPs.

Yet for most of us, that approach is unworkable. We neither can nor should allow available funds to determine our areas of concentration.

When Are Contracts the Right Vehicle?

There are times when a contract may be the best solution. For example, consider the following scenario.

Let's say that our organization has a truly outstanding hospice facility, known nationally not only for the quality of care but also for its publications and willingness to train others. We want to create a major national training center aimed at hospice facility administrators. The center would publish a newsletter, hold annual conferences, and provide an administrative hotline and onsite consultations at other facilities.

We costed out the idea and we estimate that we will need half a million dollars to do it right. Although there are some government agencies that have supported the hospice movement, none offers more than $100,000 a year for three years, and the competition for those awards is very keen.

We decide to mount an effort, beginning with our own Congressional representative, to introduce legislation in the upcoming health care appropriations bill to create a national hospice center. Concurrently, we meet with staff of the federal agency that would implement the project if funded by Congress and are able to garner their support for the bill. We meet as well with executive staff of the National Hospice Organization (NHO) and as a result propose that their involvement be written into the legislation.

Both the agency and the NHO testify before Congress that there is a need for a national training center, and as a result funds are appropriated.

The agency in turn develops an RFP that invites interested parties to bid on the center. Owing to our demonstrated expertise—and effective proposal development skills—we are awarded the contract to create the center.

Isn't That Called "Pork Barrel" Legislation?

Please distinguish the strategy used in the above scenario from some of the shenanigans that go on in Congress, for example, when a member of Congress slips into an unrelated bill language that provides funding specifically for a project in his or her district. That type of action is unfair, since it involves behind-the-scenes maneuvering instead of the open approach used by the hospice facility in the scenario above. The facility developed a sound case why and how the government should address a certain need, and it then proceeded to strive in open competition with others for the opportunity to engage in work prescribed by an agency.

A Distinction That Favors Seeking Grants

When the government issues an RFP (in the parlance, "puts a contract out on the street"), it abides by very strict rules. Although the job may be to conduct a study, say, for the Administration on Aging, the RFP is actually issued by a contracts office, and it is to this office that all inquiries must be directed. The agency itself cannot have any interaction with a potential bidder, cannot comment on the ideas being proposed, and most certainly cannot look at anything being written in response to the RFP.

By comparison, an agency conducting a grant competition can and often does interact with potential applicants (although each interaction must be initiated by an applicant). If you want to know if any idea will "fly," you can call the project officer or even go see him or her. As a result, you often can get a much clearer understanding of the types of proposals that are going to be looked upon favorably in the review process.

GETTING GOOD INFORMATION

For all of its size and complexity, the federal government is relatively accessible. Agency staff are public servants, and it is their job to provide information to callers, see potential applicants, and explain the agency's priorities. You do not need to exercise the same degree of caution as is appropriate for a private foundation, where the initial inquiry may be interpreted as a request for support (with the result that you get turned down before you've had the chance to present your case). Agency staff, then, are an excellent source of information on federal funding. Here are some others.

Catalog of Federal Domestic Assistance

The *Catalog of Federal Domestic Assistance* (*Catalog*) is a compendium of virtually every program funded by the federal government in a given year, with information on funding agencies, eligibility requirements, deadlines, funding guidelines, and who to contact.

The *Catalog* can be accessed according to cross references by agency, subject, eligibility (who can apply), and function or purpose. Each program is assigned a five-digit number. The first two numbers refer to the funding agency (the Department of Education is 84), the third number refers to the specific agency or office that conducts the funding priority being described, and the final two numbers indicate the specific program.

Here's an example taken from the 1986 edition of the *Catalog:* 84.029 is the number assigned to Special Education Personnel Development, the program that provides funding for training personnel for the education of the handicapped. The 84 indicates that this competition is administered by the Department of Education. The third digit designates the Office of the Assistant Secretary for Special Education and Rehabilitation Services, which is charged with conducting all special education competitions. The final two digits are reserved for the personnel preparation competition.

Turning to 84.029 in the *Catalog,* one will find information on the objectives and uses of this program. There is also information on the application process and who to contact. Of particular helpfulness is the section entitled "Examples of Funded Projects," which reveals that the competition has funded a range of activities within the following kinds of organizations:

- a state education agency that provides training on how to integrate children with disabilities into the regular classroom
- a university that provides masters and post-masters training
- a nonprofit educational agency that offers training to paraprofessionals
- a university that offers training to Native American teachers

It should be noted that the *Catalog* is a compendium, an inventory at a point in time. Programs added during the current fiscal year are obviously not included.

The *Federal Register*

The *Federal Register* is the federal government's vehicle for disseminating current information regarding upcoming priorities, regulations, and grant competitions. Once a bill becomes law, the agency charged with implementation may publish regulations that reflect its interpretation of the law. These may include funding priorities. For example, let's say that legislation has been passed creating regional centers for disseminating information on Alzheimer's disease. Funds have been appropriated for the upcoming fiscal year. The next step is for the proper agency, in this case the Administration on Aging, to develop regulations through which the intent of the law will be carried out.

These regulations appear in the *Federal Register,* providing readers an opportunity to comment and suggest modifications. The agency reviews all comments and publishes final regulations, often in conjunction with the announcement of a grant competition.

For organizations interested in federal funding, the *Federal Register* contains program descriptions, guidelines, criteria by which applications will be evaluated, and application procedures and formats. Whereas the *Catalog* is published annually, the *Federal Register* comes out daily. Whereas the *Catalog* provides an overview of all known programs, the *Federal Register* provides detailed information as it becomes available.

Commercial Publications

As is the case with information on private foundations, there is a ready market for information on federal agency priorities and grant competitions. Much of the information provided commercially is timely and helpful and should be considered as a practical alternative to ploughing through publications such as the *Federal Register.*

HOW TO OBTAIN FEDERAL SUPPORT

Let's apply some of what we know about marketing strategies to the task of securing federal grant or contract support.

Segment the Market

There are over one thousand grant programs described each year in the *Catalog,* and these are administered by some fifty different agencies. But it is not very difficult to winnow that one thousand down to a manageable handful.

Contact your professional association, if you belong to one, and ask for the agencies that would be most reasonable for you to contact. Be sure to get the name and phone number of an agency staff person. If it can be determined that there is someone from your profession working for that agency, so much the better: He or she will have at least a basic understanding of what you want to accomplish.

Make use of some of the work done for you in order to separate out the best prospects. Among print sources, the *Annual Register of Grant Support,* the *Directory of Biomedical and Health Care Grants,* and the *Guide to*

Federal Funding in Education allow you to access information according to subject and also to see who has gotten agency funding the previous year.

Information is now also readily available via computerized data bases, such as SPIN and Dialog. For those interested in general grant opportunities, there is Comserve, and for those interested in special education, SpecialNet. (Each of these data bases requires a subscription fee, and there is an online charge for actual use. Information on how to contact the data bases can be found in the resources section at the end of this chapter.)

The chances are very strong that your organization either subscribes to one of these data bases or has access to one. If not, you may want to look to your professional association or even your alma mater.

Let's take a closer look at one of the electronic data bases, SPIN, in order to see the kind of information that can be obtained.

SPIN is maintained by the State University of New York (SUNY) Research Foundation. It has some three thousand funding listings, covering both public and private sector sources across the country. Information can be accessed according to research or training grants along ten major key word classifiers, including health, medical science, and science and technology.

Information can be displayed on your computer screen and printed out as it appears or you can request that "batches" of information be printed out from the central computer and mailed to you. Funding information will include the "sponsor" (funding agency), the address and telephone number, the titles of programs being funded, the deadlines for submission of proposals, the purpose of the programs, information on who may apply, and estimated dollars available.

As an alternative to tracking the *Federal Register,* SPIN provides a weekly update of agency announcements as well as listings of RFPs.

Determine Your Best Chances

The personnel preparation grant competition that is conducted annually by the Office of Special Education Programs and Rehabilitative Services was mentioned above. It is referred to in the *Catalog* by the number 84.029.

Within that program there are several specific competitions. Some have a funding ratio—the ratio of proposals funded to proposals received—of 1:3. Some have a ratio as high as 1:17. Obviously, all things being equal, you stand a much better chance of being funded in a competition with a low funding ratio.

How do you find out the ratio for each competition? Ask the project officer who coordinates the program you're interested in.

Position Your Program

See Chapter 13 for some thoughts on making your program generally more visible. For now, consider the following ways of becoming better known within the federal sector:

- Volunteer to serve as a proposal reviewer. You'll become better known to the funding agency, learn how the proposal review system works from the inside, and see firsthand what makes a winning proposal.
- Respond to draft priorities included in the *Federal Register* in areas related to your program.
- Get to know people who have been funded by the agency that you're targeting. This may lead to an opportunity for collaboration with an individual who has a proven track record.

Match Needs to Solutions

Federal agencies tell you what their needs are in the form of agency priorities. For your proposal to be successful, it must demonstrate how you can address one or more of those needs. Be sure you understand what the agency is looking for. Share your ideas with agency project staff before committing them to paper in the form of a lengthy proposal.

Companies that survive on government grants or contracts may have a win ratio of no better than 1:5, and the ratio is often closer to 1:10. That's true in part because they are typically less selective than you will be. Although they also segment the universe of agencies to determine where best to submit proposals, they are in the business of responding to RFPs and grant announcements and are not against taking an occasional long shot in order to expand their market.

You will frequently see executives of such companies in the halls of federal agencies meeting with agency staff in order to learn about upcoming grant or contract opportunities or to get "debriefed" regarding a proposal they submitted that did not get funded.

Perseverance

You would not want to live or die based on whether you got a federal grant. Applying for support is stress producing and the chances of success are often slim. But you probably could use a little of the aggressiveness with which some firms go after funds. They stay with it, knowing that they will learn from mistakes and hit the jackpot on enough proposals to succeed as a business.

Imagination

You might also consider the willingness of some firms to expand into new areas. Many programs tend to look for federal support from one department—and often just one agency within that department. For example, a program might go back time and again to the Department of Education, yet some of what it does might well fit the priorities of the Department of Health and Human Services.

You need to strike a balance, segmenting the market into the best prospects while not overlooking hidden opportunities.

RESOURCES

Listed below are the addresses to which to send for details on electronic data bases that provide funding information.

Comserve
Department of Language, Literature and Communication
Sage Laboratories
Rensselaer Polytechnic Institute
Troy, NY 12180

Dialog
Dialog Information Services, Inc.
3460 Hillview Avenue
Palo Alto, CA 94304

SpecialNet
National Association of State Directors of Special Education
2021 K Street, N.W.
Washington, DC 20006

SPIN
Sponsored Programs Information Network
The Research Foundation of SUNY
Albany, NY 12201

Chapter 10

Characteristics of a Good Proposal

One need not be a professional grantsman to write the kind of proposal that results in funding, but a well-organized writing plan is essential. . . . The key to effective proposal writing . . . lies in breaking the proposal into manageable sections . . . and then using logic and plain language to explain, step-by-step, exactly what you want to do, why, and how.

Nolan Estes
Consultant, Radio Shack

Developing a successful proposal is no more—and no less—than marketing your ideas. The written proposal is an integral part of the marketing plan in much the same way that an advertising and selling strategy is an integral part of selling products. It is possible that a very good product will find a market by virtue of its worth. It is much more likely that a product, perhaps of lesser worth, will find a market as the result of an effective marketing strategy.

WHAT MAKES A PROPOSAL GOOD?

For starters, we need to make clear that, at least in this context, "good" means successful or fundable (or, better still, funded). The merit of a proposal depends mainly, not on the value of the ideas, but on how well the ideas are presented to the funding agency. In other words, the issue here is not solely good ideas but good presentation of ideas. A lot of good ideas have never been realized—yours and mine among them—because they were never effectively articulated to the right agency. They were not converted into good proposals.

A Case in Point

Barry Nicklesberg, Executive Director of the Funding Center in Washington, D.C., was known to claim that he could get anything funded by writing a good proposal—anything. Someone questioned that boast and a small wager was made. His challenger suggested that Nicklesberg secure funding to determine "why monkeys click their teeth," confident that the idea was so absurd that no one would fund it.

Wrong. Nicklesberg wrote what proved to be a winning proposal for the National Science Foundation and was awarded funds for a study entitled "Why Monkeys Click Their Teeth." (The proposal also had the dubious achievement of being selected by Senator William Proxmire for one of his famous Golden Fleece awards, which he presented to federally funded projects that he considered ridiculous and a waste of taxpayer money.)

Did the idea have merit? Probably not. But was the proposal good? Apparently so. At least if we define a good proposal as one that gets funded. The fact that the proposal also won a Golden Fleece award only further dramatizes the subjectivity of proposal assessments. What's good for one agency, one funding source, or one proposal reader may not be what someone with a different set of interests and criteria would consider good.

CREATING A GOOD PROPOSAL

Know Thy Funder

In marketing terms, developing a good proposal begins with a knowledge of the marketplace. Effective research into the wants and interests of the potential funder will greatly increase your chances of success. Marketing and management guru Peter Drucker puts it this way: "The aim of marketing is to make selling superfluous. The aim is to know the customer so well that the product or service fits him and sells itself."[1]

Thus, what interests the National Science Foundation may be of little or no interest to the Department of Labor, the Spencer Foundation, or the officer in charge of corporate giving for Megabucks Ltd. in your own town. In the example above, Barry Nicklesberg was able to develop a fundable proposal because he found a funding source that fit the topic at hand, an agency that would be interested in a well-crafted proposal having to do with animal behavior research. For that particular agency, a seemingly esoteric question such as why monkeys click their teeth (if in fact they do) was not outside the realm of inquiry. Doing research to try to answer it may have provided some information on aggressive behavior, for example. So although the topic was absurd in the eyes of Senator Proxmire—and indeed in the eyes of Nicklesberg and his challenger—it may have been viewed as worthy of study (and worthy of funding) by someone with an interest in animal behavior.

Understanding Motivation

Knowing your funder requires that you understand the motivations and behavior of the particular funding source, be it public or private, an individual or a company. It requires that you consider your idea from the perspective of that potential funder. What interests the agency? What can you learn about the key players who establish its funding priorities? How do they think?

A certain federal agency, let's call it Agency X, is headed by a person of extraordinary intelligence, someone who thinks in terms of large "conceptual frameworks" around which projects are designed. If you were thinking of submitting a proposal to this agency, it would behoove you to consider your ideas in relation to these conceptual frameworks, perhaps even sharing your ideas with the agency while they are still in the formative stages. This is not to say that you would get direct help in developing a proposal, but you might well get help in shaping an idea such that the proposal you ultimately submit to the agency would have a better chance of success.

By comparison, a large New York foundation, call it Foundation Y, was formed by a person who was a senior budget staff person in the Nixon administration and whose economic views are fiscally conservative. The foundation which he formed supports studies and demonstration projects having to do with reimbursement for health services.

Although it may not be fair to prejudge, it is unlikely that this foundation would support a proposal that advocated a national health plan under which everyone's health needs would be entirely covered. The foundation might, however, be favorably inclined toward a proposal to study how costs could be cut by training people as multiskilled health practitioners.

Recognizing the Differences among Funders

Determining *where* to submit your proposal is as important as what to say. We're talking not only about understanding funders—knowing what makes them tick—but also about understanding the difference among types of funders.

To begin with, deciding where to submit is a matter of determining the priorities of the various funding sources, both public and private. Such information is readily available commercially and also through your development office (or the office of sponsored programs).

Knowing your funder is also a matter of understanding the differences between public and private sector sources (and among sources of each kind as well). Many federal agencies, for example, prefer to fund projects that seem to have national impact. Since they have limited resources, they often look for projects that seem likely to have an impact beyond the borders of Outback, Montana.

Within the federal government itself there is a wide range of funding behavior. For example, the Administration on Aging (AoA) and the National Institute of Aging (NIA) would seem to share common ground; indeed, they are both vitally interested in the nation's elderly. However, AoA leans more toward gerontology, NIA toward geriatrics; NIA supports the work of medical and allied fields, whereas AoA has supported and helped build a network of centers that serve the social and economic needs of older Americans.

Even on a philosophical level, federal agencies differ. Some, such as the Fund for the Improvement of Postsecondary Education, are willing to take risks, to try out new approaches. Others look to the track record of the person or organization submitting the proposal, giving as much weight to it as to the proposal itself.

As different as federal agencies are from each other, they are remarkably alike when contrasted with private foundations. Federal agencies, by virtue of the fact that they are public, are accessible. They publish information on their priorities, they are open to appointments with persons who want to discuss proposal ideas, and they can even provide guidance as to the nuances within their priorities.

Understanding the behavior, motivation, and interests of private foundations begins with a recognition that they are indeed private. While private foundations are becoming more accessible, they are in general much more closed than their public sector counterparts, preferring to respond to a proposal in hand rather than to meet to discuss an idea.

Among smaller foundations, priorities are likely to have been derived either from the wishes of the foundation's major donor or his or her family. Such foundations, and they are in the majority, do not have large staffs, and indeed some have no paid staff at all. Also, in choosing proposals they tend to be more subjective and may rely more on the applicant's reputation and on statements of recommendations.

Getting Funders To Know You

Within larger foundations, staff often play a more pivotal role in determining priorities and selecting recipients. Board members determine overall policy but tend to respect the opinions of staff. And staff as a rule are reasonably accessible: It is, after all, their job to represent the foundation and respond to inquiries about it.

Foundation staffers are also interested in presenting and sometimes even being spokespersons for what they feel are meritorious projects. They have an investment in the ability of their foundation to accomplish good works and can play a critical role in shaping ideas into proposals that will appeal to the voting board members. They may in turn be judged by the proposals that they bring forth and support. If they consistently present high-quality ideas, that reflects well on their own judgment and certainly does no harm to their careers.

It follows, then, that getting to know staff people on larger foundations is of potential benefit to your program. How do you go about making yourself known? You could call with ideas that, based on your research, seem to fit solidly with the foundation's interests. Of course, you should listen to the advice you receive and adhere to it as best you can. You might also try to involve staff members in your program, perhaps as speakers at a seminar or as commentors on a paper that you are developing on a topic of mutual interest.

As with any relationship, you shouldn't force it. You will succeed with the staffs of some foundations and not with others. But getting yourself known by even one foundation is not a bad start.

How do you get to know your funder if it is a small foundation? Get to know a key player. Who in your organization or associated with it might know a member of the board? What might you do to get yourself introduced so that your proposal does not so readily blend in with the hundreds of others? Is it possible to arrange for a brief meeting with the foundation staff or one of the board members prior to actually submitting your application? Can you at least use the name of a contact person in calling to try out an idea or in the cover letter accompanying your proposal?

You should not seek to exert undue influence or put pressure on the foundation to support you because of whom you know. Rather, you should merely seek a chance to be heard, or chance to present a proposal that can stand on its own merits if it gets a fair hearing. You are also looking for some friendly advice as to whether your idea fits the foundation's interests and whether there might some way to tailor it so that it still meets your needs while accommodating the needs of the donor. In Drucker's words, you are looking for a means to make the selling of your proposal superfluous.

Imagine yourself as the funding agency to which you are submitting a proposal. What are all the reasons they might not want to fund your project? Your proposal needs to address these positively.

Know Thyself

Consider the following remarks by Thomas James, a past president of the Spencer Foundation:

> One of the most persistent questions we have had to deal with . . . , put to us in a variety of ways, comes down to "What do you want us to do?"
> Given the high value we place on question finding, there is only one answer to that question: "Not a thing!"—though we too vary the phrasing. With our conviction that inner-directed scholars . . . are most likely to come up with the best questions for research, we find little time for those who wonder what they might do to attract our funds: let the question come first, and then if we can, we will try to reward it.[2]

The Spencer Foundation operates with a relatively small staff but has nonetheless made an impact through funding studies related to cognition, early childhood development, and the development of language. It has decided that as a funder it can do its job most effectively not by trying to steer applicants in a particular direction but rather by being responsive to those who come in with a good idea. And unresponsive to those who don't.

Know What Makes Your Program Special

The first rule, then, in dealing with the Spencer Foundation, or with virtually any potential funder, is to know yourself. By now you should be able to articulate what it is that your program can do well, what makes it unique, and why it merits the attention of a foundation or other kind of funder.

Be Realistic

The second rule is to be realistic about what your program can and cannot do. Here you can refer to the work that you've done to assess your program's strengths and weaknesses and its potential. Knowing what you can do well is fundamental to successful proposal writing for two reasons:

1. Proposal reviewers are by and large a jaded lot. They have been chosen for their knowledge and expertise, and they know what's been done and what's realistic. To catch their attention you need to present something that is not only innovative but workable. If you are unrealistic about what you can get accomplished, that will be reflected in the proposal and picked up by the reviewers.
2. Your proposed scope of work needs to match your credentials. If your proposal is for a major study in health care reimbursement but there is no record of experience in this area among those described in the section on personnel, you are not likely to be awarded the grant.

Be Imaginative

If you want to conduct that study on health care reimbursement but don't have the credentials, you can do some background work that will make your proposal believable:

- Exhaust the literature on the topic.
- Hire someone who has knowledge of the topic and has been funded before to help write your proposal.
- Establish an expert advisory team whose credentials will be listed in the personnel section of your proposal.

- Indicate that you will hire, for example, a project director with the type of skills necessary to manage a study on health care reimbursement.
- Link up with another department or with another institution. Who has been getting funded in this area? Could you submit a joint proposal?
- Demonstrate why your program is a good choice. You may not know much about conducting a major reimbursement study, but you can speak with authority about patient care, reimbursement practices within a sample setting (your own), and the problems presented by limited reimbursement.

Crystallize Your Thinking

Before you set fingers to keyboard, be sure you can state exactly what it is you want to accomplish. If you cannot state this within one sentence, you may not have refined your idea far enough. You may be trying to do too much.

A GOOD PROPOSAL: ESSENTIAL ELEMENTS

OK. You know what it is that you want to accomplish if funded, and you have selected a potential funding source. Now on to writing the proposal. Although both the content and, to some degree, the format of every proposal will differ, there are essential elements common to all winning proposals.

Abstract

Most federal agencies require a one-page abstract, which they use in compiling summaries of funded projects. It is also used by proposal readers as a kind of advance organizer: It proves much easier to wade through an extensive proposal when one has an idea of what it is all about. Thus the abstract, although not usually evaluated explicitly, plays an important role. It needs to capture the best elements of your proposal—the need that will be addressed, the means that will be used—in about 250 words or less.

Should you write the abstract before or after the proposal itself? Both. If you cannot crystallize your thinking into a few words, at most a few sentences, you probably need to step back and rethink what it is you want to accomplish. You may not have narrowed the scope of work to a manageable size or not sufficiently have tightened the focus on the objectives you want to attain. Writing the abstract first will help to determine whether you do know—and can say briefly—what the need is and what you want to do about it.

The abstract should then be reviewed after the proposal is completed. Is it an accurate reflection of what is contained in the longer document? Have you made some shifts in the scope of work that necessitate modifying the abstract?

Statement of Need

The statement of need (sometimes entitled "Extent of Need," "Significance," "Problem Statement," or "Needs Assessment") is a pivotal part of the proposal for two reasons:

1. It comes early in the proposal, often being the first portion of the narrative to be read by the reviewer. If it reads well, if it convincingly presents a need, the reviewer is going to be in the right frame of mind to learn how you plan to deal with the need. If it is not convincing, no plan of operation is going to make the reader believe this is a proposal worth funding.
2. It often weighs heavily in the overall evaluation. Most proposals can receive a maximum score of 100; the statement of need may account for a quarter of that total.

What makes a statement of need compelling?

- It relates to the interests and priorities of the funding agency to whom the proposal is being submitted.
- It presents a problem that is important to address but not so large that no project could feasibly address it.
- If submitted to a federal agency or major foundation, it addresses a problem of regional if not national significance.
- The need is well documented: There is an analysis of relevant literature, there are substantiating statistical data, and there is evidence that the project would help those most affected by the problem.

It must be clear to the potential funding source that the need does not exist only in the mind of the applicant. Some proposals never get funded because the reviewers perceive correctly that the proposal is too self-serving; it would be good for the applicant but not necessarily for anyone else.

Here, according to one foundation official, is what reviewers look for:

Is this type of project an activity that fits within the foundation's program interests? . . . Can [the project] serve as an experiment that has transferral potential? Is it addressed to a need that other organizations are also feeling? . . . The project may have an intrinsic value of its own from which others will benefit. To phrase this in question form: Is this project of importance to society at large?[3]

Objectives

The statement of objectives, in some proposal formats, is included as part of the statement of need or the section on methodology. In any case, the presentation of objectives should be a logical bridge between the discussion of needs and methods. Having presented a sound statement of need, the proposal then indicates the objectives that will be accomplished in order to lessen the need or reduce the problem. The section on methodology is then an explication of those objectives.

What makes a statement of objectives effective?

- The objectives are presented in measurable terms.
- They are presented as results and not as the means to attain those results.
- There is a direct correlation between the needs and objectives: If there are three needs stated, there should be a corresponding number of objectives.
- Where appropriate, the objectives suggest some time frame.

Norman Bell and Frank Jackson, authors of *Radio Shack's Proposal Writing Guide,* suggest that the writer answer the following questions in developing a statement of objectives:

1. Who is target group of the project?
2. What will the target group be receiving or doing?
3. How long will the receiving or doing last?
4. What will be the result?
5. How will you know if the result has been achieved?[4]

Plan of Operation

The plan of operation (sometimes entitled "Methods," "Methodology," "Scope of Work," or, in research proposals, "Technical Soundness" or "Experimental Design and Methods") details the efforts that will be directed toward meeting the objectives and thus mitigating the problem described in the statement of need. The staff of one federal agency noted that the plan of operation serves to "improve the understanding of how a grant, if supported, will be administered. The Plan of Operation must illustrate how the effective management of scarce resources will be made available to meet the various objectives of the agencies submitting the application, and in particular, the objectives of the federally supported portion of the program."[5]

Picture the finished proposal as a chain, each link leading to the next, each a logical sequel to the one before. All links are connected, so that if one link fails, the chain fails. If there are two problems, there should be two major objectives. The explication of how these two objectives will be achieved then forms the narrative of the plan of operation. It should be clear to the reader that implementing the plan will have a direct impact on the problems.

Consider the following when developing a plan of operation:

- The plan should present an orderly sequence of events, often both in narrative and chart form.
- The selection of activities to be undertaken should make sense, that is, the activities constitute a logical way of getting the job done.
- The work proposed should be accomplishable within the indicated time frame.

The plan of operation may also be the place to describe who is going to do the work, that is, not the background or experience of the personnel but rather how the work will be divided among them. This may be presented in either narrative or chart form.

You might want to consider two charts. One chart has the time frame indicated across the top and the tasks noted down the side (Figure 10-1). The second is a modified organizational chart that indicates relationships between the various members of the project team (Figure 10-2).

Evaluation

Not every proposal will have a separate section on evaluation. Some funding agencies may request that an evaluation plan be included within the plan of operation, to which it relates; some agencies make no mention of evaluation at all. Whether mentioned or not, the evaluation component is essential for virtually any proposal methodology. It should be built into the way you conduct a project, and its incorporation in the proposal gives some assurance to the reviewer that progress will be made according to stated objectives.

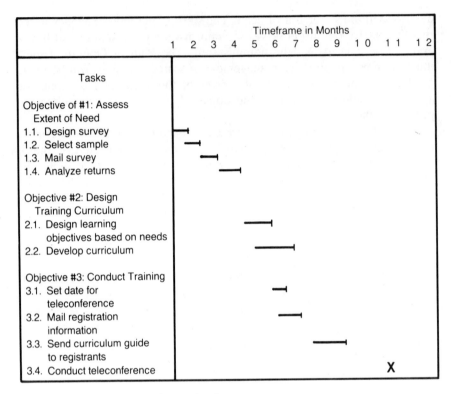

Figure 10-1 Project Schedule (Abbreviated)

The evaluation plan is seldom assigned many points and does not need to be lengthy; in fact, the section can suffer from overkill. The following comments may be of help:

- There should be evidence of a plan by which the project will measure the degree to which the objectives are being achieved.

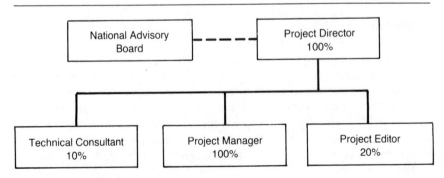

Figure 10-2 Organizational Chart

- That plan should contain both formative (ongoing) and summative evaluation components.
- There must be a clear indication of who will be conducting the evaluation. Although it is neither necessary not desirable to hire someone to evaluate the project, the evaluation measures do need to provide an objective look at how well the project is progressing.
- Where appropriate (for example, with a research proposal), the evaluation plan should describe the data that will be collected and the means by which they will be analyzed.

Key Personnel

The section on key personnel is integral to a good proposal, and in some cases it is the most important section. Those evaluating it will want to know four things:

1. Does the person identified as the project director (or "principal investigator," as she or he might be called in a research proposal) have the educational background, experience, and knowledge to undertake the proposed scope of work?
2. Do other members of the proposed project team have appropriate credentials as well? These other members may complement the capabilities of the project director. For example, the project director may have an excellent background in gerontology and bring someone in as part of the proposal team with an in-depth knowledge of management information systems.
3. Is there a match between the duties assigned to the key personnel and their backgrounds? Some applicant organizations make the mistake of prominently mentioning people who have impressive credentials but who will actually play a minuscule role in the project.
4. Are the key players involved committing an amount of time to the project that is sufficient to get the work done without being excessive?

Here is how the staff of one agency described the kind of section on key personnel that would merit all of the points available for that section: "The qualifications of the Project Director and other key personnel are fully outlined showing relevant training and experience which are appropriate for the roles they will perform in accomplishing the goals of the project. Activities and time commitments of project personnel are clear and consistent with the overall goals of the project."[6]

By comparison, a proposal might receive minimal points if it fails to provide specific information on the staffing that "will be needed for the project, their roles, relevant experience and professional backgrounds."[7]

Adequacy of Resources

Most funding sources will want to know not only about the key personnel assigned to the project but also about the organization submitting the proposal. What experience does it bring to the proposed project? What resources (for example, office space, computer equipment, and accounting support) will it provide? How old is the organization, what are its mission and goals, and in what other pertinent activities is it engaged?

Budget

In most federal grant proposals, the budget is considered a fundamental element, receiving as much as 10 percent of the total points awarded. What makes a sound budget?

- The budget parallels the proposal narrative: One can go back and forth between the two and easily discern the interrelationships.
- It is in sufficient detail to demonstrate that the applicant knows how much this project is really going to cost.
- It indicates the project costs that will be borne by the applicant organization or by some other funding source.
- There is an accompanying narrative that describes how costs were derived. For example, "The travel estimate of $750 is based on one round-trip coach fare at $400, three days per diem at $100, and $50 for ground transportation to and from the sites under study as well as transportation to and from the airport."
- The costs are reasonable—sufficient for the project without being "padded."

The scope and complexity of the budgetary details will depend on the funding agency and the type of award. Private sector funders tend to require less detailed budgets than government agencies, and the latter generally require a more detailed budget for contracts as opposed to grants. Determining how large the budget can be will be influenced by three factors:

1. The first factor, of course, is the determination of what is actually required to complete the project. Don't underbudget in order to "come in low" in the hope of getting points; a skilled reviewer will see that you cannot do the work for the money requested.
2. With RFPs and most grants announcements, a ceiling figure will be indicated. In the case of RFPs, this is often expressed in person-years, which are each roughly the equivalent of 75,000 to 100,000 dollars.

3. Where no such fixed ceiling is given, as may be the case with a private foundation, a look at the past two or three years of the foundation's grant activity will yield a range and average amount.

Additional Elements

Beyond these basic elements, there are some which may be required, depending on the funding sources.

Impact

Particularly for a federal proposal, it may be important to indicate the impact this project will have nationally if it is successfully implemented. The agency may ask for some specifics here, for example, numbers of persons that will ultimately benefit. The impact section is the counterpart of the statement of need. If the project achieves its objectives, it will have a meaningful impact on the problem that motivated the project.

Future Funding

Private sector funders are especially interested in how the work will continue after the grant period. They want to be assured not only that the work will continue but that the applicant organization is not going to rely on them for that continuation. If the project being proposed is ongoing, and you are looking for start-up funds, it will be necessary to demonstrate that you have some plan for continuation and to indicate whether in the long run you will depend on institutional funds, third party payments, fees to clients or students, or another funding agency.

Dissemination

In some proposals, dissemination may be an intrinsic element; if it is, it will likely be weighted heavily. For example, let's imagine you are developing a proposal for a project that would provide information on educational intervention strategies for teachers working with learning disabled children. You are going to gather articles on this subject that have already been published, organize them according to subtopic, and then compile the materials into a book of readings.

If your dissemination plan is deficient, the proposal has little to offer. The project is only as good as its ability to get the materials into the right hands.

HOW DOES A PROPOSAL GET REVIEWED?

Understanding what will happen to your proposal once it is submitted is fundamental to understanding the funded agency.

Federal Grant Review Process

The proposal that you submit typically goes first, not to the agency that will fund it, but to a proposal clearinghouse, where it is "logged in" to document that it was received on time. It is then forwarded to the appropriate agency, in particular, to the staff person (sometimes referred to as the "competition manager") who is charged with coordinating the review process.

The manager has by this time identified and made contact with knowledgeable individuals outside the government who have agreed to serve on a review panel. The reviewers may be sent the proposals (they may read somewhere between 10 and 20) in advance, but more commonly they will not receive them until they arrive in Washington for the review "impaneling." In most instances, there will be three persons assigned to a review team, and their job is to evaluate each proposal according to criteria provided by the agency. These criteria have been published in the *Federal Register* as part of the initial announcement of the grant competition. Table 10-1 provides the criteria used for one agency within the Department of Education.

Having read the proposals independently of one another, the review panelists then meet together with the competition manager or other staff to review their rankings and evaluations. At this time individual reviewers have an opportunity to indicate why they scored a certain proposal as they did, and their colleagues on the panel have a chance to consider whether to modify their own scoring in light of such information.

The individual scores are averaged, and a summary commentary on each proposal is prepared during this panel meeting. The panelists may be given an opportunity to indicate which proposals they unqualifiedly recommend for funding, which they recommend if certain changes are made, and which they do not recommend.

The results from each of the panels are then combined to determine the total ranking. Agency staff then make their recommendations as to which

Table 10-1 Sample Proposal Review Criteria

Criteria	Rating
Importance	(0–10)
Technical Soundness	(0–40)
Plan of Operation	(0–10)
Evaluation Plan	(0–5)
Quality of Key Personnel	(0–10)
Adequacy of Resources	(0–5)
Budget and Cost Effectiveness	(0–5)
Total Rating	(0–100)

proposals should be considered for funding. The process continues up the line until the head of the agency signs off.

Before the awards are actually made, the winning proposals are forwarded to a grants and contracts office to make sure that all expenditures are allowable. There may be negotiations with the applicant on certain expenditures or on certain aspects of the proposed scope of work prior to the formal notification of award.

Private Sector Grant Review Process

Although their giving patterns are less diverse than they once were, foundations and other private sector sources do not always follow the relatively orderly process of federal agencies. As was mentioned earlier, decision making as performed by foundations tends to vary by size of foundation, by type and size of staff, and by whim. Corporate donors, while becoming more aware of their role in preserving the private sector, are nonetheless tied to their own product line and its marketing strategy.

According to one private foundation principal, the review process within foundations is often as follows:

1. The proposal is screened to determine whether there is sufficient information, whether the applicant holds the necessary tax status (typically 501(c)(3)), and whether the proposal generally seems to "fit."
2. Usually the next step is to gather additional information through interviews, library research, use of consultants, and, occasionally, site visits.
3. The information is analyzed by some combination of staff, consultants, board members, and the advisory committee. The analysis may consider the following:
   - What is the projected timetable and budget?
   - Is there a real need for the project?
   - Is the project duplicative of other projects, especially those already being funded?
   - Is the evaluation plan sufficient?
   - What plans are included for funding after the initial grant?
4. The analysis is compiled into a memo (or record) regarding the applicant. This memo provides factual background information for the board's consideration, and it may include
   - general data on the applicant
   - relevant budget information (for example, information about whether the applicant is fiscally sound)
   - a record of any previous funding of the applicant by the foundation

- an evaluation of the project according to the priorities of the foundation
- recommendations

5. The board then meets and decides on the applications that have been received. These meetings may be frequent or infrequent and with or without staff. Most large foundations have such meetings at least quarterly.[8]

WHY PROPOSALS FAIL

Why do proposals fail? The reasons vary from funding agency to funding agency, of course, but, putting aside the subjective elements, there are certain prevalent factors that cause proposals not to get funded:

- Some proposals are not in the required format. Nothing is more frustrating to a proposal reader than to have to rank a proposal low that has some very good ideas but does not state them in accordance with the agency's review criteria.
- Some are too ambitious, proposing to undertake a scope of work in two years that couldn't be accomplished in four.
- Applicants sometimes misunderstand the funding agency's priorities. This is not all that hard to do: Private foundations don't always make their priorities known, and some government agencies appear to have field tested their application kits to be sure they are confusing.
- Sometimes it is clear that the applicant is "shotgunning" proposals, that is, sending essentially the same proposal to several potential funding sources. The result is doubly negative: The proposal doesn't get funded because it doesn't really fit, and the reviewer is left with a negative impression of the applicant.

George Eaves, a scientist with the National Institutes of Health (NIH), has suggested several factors leading to the demise of research proposals:

- absence of innovative ideas
- a research plan that lacks focus
- an ineffective methodology
- unconvincing presentation of relevant literature[9]

HOW TO SUCCEED

There is no assurance that even the best-crafted proposal will be funded, but the odds of being successful will increase exponentially for the program that follows these guidelines:

1. By way of review: Be sure you know the agency to whom you are submitting the proposal. That includes knowing the past ratio of proposals funded to proposals received. If the ratio is much higher than 1:10, you may want to consider another source.
2. Submit to agencies where you can build a strong case for funding, for example, where you or someone on your proposal team knows the topic and where you can establish a credible record of experience.
3. Give yourself enough time. Don't forget the time that will be required for writing, rewriting, word processing, duplication, and collation, and schedule enough time to get signatures and approvals.
4. Be succinct. Proposal readers often have other things they want to do with their time, as hard as this is to believe. If a reader is plodding through your proposal at 2:00 A.M. after having spent the day at the Cherry Blossom Festival, make it easy for him or her by being brief and to the point.
5. Provide an index or table of contents keyed to the evaluation criteria. The idea, again, is to make reviewing your proposal an easy task.
6. Follow the directions of the agency to which you are applying. If the agency calls the plan of operation the "Materiel Fulfillment Control," you call it that, too.
7. Have your proposal "field tested" if possible; ask someone whose judgment you value to read it in draft and evaluate it according to the agency's criteria.
8. Believe in yourself. If you think the proposal is a bad idea, it will be.

Learning how to write a competitive proposal takes some practice, but the results in terms of what it allows you to do with your program will make the time well spent. As one veteran proposal writer put it,

> The primary value of writing a proposal, and another proposal, and yet another proposal, is that each successive one sharpens your understanding of your ideas. . . . Experienced faculty members who receive lots of grants generally have proposal-success ratios smaller than would be condoned by those who elect not to apply—but they do as well receive more money. They do not subscribe to the view that writing an unfunded proposal is a bad use of time. They use what they've learned to make it work better the next time.[10]

This writer's comments are borne out by the facts. A study by the National Science Foundation found that applicants for research grants improved their chances for funding dramatically by revising and resubmitting their applications. The study found that one out of every four persons who took the time to resubmit was funded the second time around. Yet almost half of those who did not get funded decided not to resubmit at all.[11] The point is that those who took the additional time to find out what was lacking in their proposal in order to improve it often ended up winning a grant, including those who had never before been funded by the agency that ultimately approved their proposal.

NOTES

1. Peter Drucker, *Management: Tasks, Responsibilities, Practices* (New York: Harper & Row, 1973), 64–65.

2. Thomas James, *Annual Report of the Spencer Foundation* (Chicago: Spencer Foundation, 1980), 3.

3. Robert A. Mayer, "What Will a Foundation Look for When You Submit a Grant Proposal," *The Foundation Center Information Quarterly*, October 1972.

4. Norman T. Bell and Frank Jackson, *Radio Shack's Proposal Writing Guide* (Dallas: Radio Shack, 1980), 40.

5. M. Angele Thomas and Doris J. Sutherland, *An Analysis of the "Plan of Operation" and "Quality of Key Personnel" Criteria in Grant Applications under Training Personnel for the Education of the Handicapped* (Reston, Va.: Council for Exceptional Children, Teacher Education Division, February 1987), 6.

6. Ibid., 2.

7. Ibid., 3.

8. Mary Hall, *Getting Funded: A Complete Guide to Proposal Writing, Third Edition.* (Portland, Oregon: Continuing Education Publications, Portland State University, 1988): 151.

9. George Eaves, quoted in "Grants Workshop: In Grantseeking, Persistence Pays Off," *Federal Grants and Contracts Weekly* 12 (January 25, 1988): 8.

10. Robert Fleischer, "Proposing a New Attitude toward Writing Proposals," Letter to the Editor, *Chronicle of Higher Education* 28 (March 24, 1982): 36.

11. "Grants Workshop: In Grantseeking, Persistence Pays Off," 1, 7.

Chapter 11

Raising Funds without Fund Raising

Basically it should be recognized that earning and receiving money means in some way the rendering of a service. . . . When we have something potentially useful or of service, we are permitted to develop that current flow of money as an expense incurred.

Ernest Goodryder
How to Earn Money as a Consultant

Although we have emphasized, in this workshop in print, the importance of being able to effectively seek grants or obtain other financial support through so-called fund raising, grant seeking and fund raising are not the only ways in which you can raise money for your program. Nor are they always the best.

In marketing terms, you have a product line—or will be developing one—that meets the needs and interests of a range of buyers. Some buyers, such as clients or students, purchase your product directly on a fee-for-service basis; others, such as private foundations and government agencies, are in effect purchasing the services on behalf of the direct users.

In developing ways of raising funds without fund raising, the focus is on the first of these two models, that is, providing a direct service or product for a fee. In some instances this may mean simply expanding the market in which services or products are offered; in other instances it may require the development of new products and services, or at least modification of existing ones.

PRODUCTS

There are several types of products that can profitably be developed by your program. We will consider three: publications, software, and equipment.

Publications

If you are a capable clinician, a talented teacher, or a rigorous researcher, chances are you have something to say that could be captured in print for a wider distribution.

Writing for Colleagues

Take a close look at some of the texts that you use in your teaching or refer to in your clinical practice. You will find, if you have not discovered this already, that much of what is contained there is information that you already knew. It may be new to a student but is largely familiar to you.

What the authors and editors have done is to "package" information, either by writing the book themselves or by compiling and editing the work of others. Rarely does information appear in a text that has not already been published or said elsewhere, for example, in scientific journals, in previous texts, or in texts from related or even unrelated fields. Writers and editors of texts provide a service that their colleagues are willing to pay for:

- They may cast knowledge into the framework of a new theory.
- They may bring information together that previously only existed in separate articles.
- They may—and hopefully they do—bring information together in a way that is fresh and cogent and interesting.

The point is that you probably know more about your field or some aspect of it than you give yourself credit for. You know you know more, but you just haven't given yourself the time to get it down on paper.

Developing a publication can enhance the resources of your program. There are several different ways (or combinations of ways) that you might proceed:

- You could develop the text yourself, on your own time, in which case your program would benefit from the prestige of a published text in the field. However, it would not directly benefit from the income, unless of course you assigned it some portion of the royalties.
- You could develop the text as a product of your department, drawing on the help of others within it. In this case, the royalities would accrue to the program directly.
- You could seek institutional funding or a small grant to underwrite release time or to pay yourself and others to tackle the material outside of work.
- You could link up with individuals in other departments, with the understanding that an equitable percentage of royalties would accrue to each department.

Writing for Noncolleagues

OK, you're not comfortable with the idea of writing for colleagues and students. You don't buy the idea that maybe you know more than you think you know. Or perhaps you are convinced that there are too many texts now on the market. Or, again, you may like the idea of developing a publication but feel that starting with a professional text is a bit overwhelming.

If you're not at ease with the idea of a professional text, what might you develop that would be of use to laypersons? How about a series of booklets explaining your own department and what it does in a way that could be used in other institutions for recruitment of prospective clients or patients or their families?

If your field is psychology, how about a folder that explains to parents the normal developmental milestones? Or how to relate to teens?

Have you done any work in infant care or geriatrics that would be of interest to prospective mothers and fathers or to adults with aging parents?

Could you develop a pamphlet on noise reduction and hearing loss that could be used by employers in your community?

How about something on safe and effective dieting, common childhood illnesses, the family's role in dealing with a person who has Alzheimer's disease, the use of hospices, public speaking, or how to select a home computer?

The list can be as long as your imagination will allow. Take a look at your syllabus or at the topics that you've covered in grand rounds or heard about in a recent workshop. Which elements could be extracted, recast, and presented to some segment of the lay public?

Keep in mind that the development of a publication follows the same rules as the development of other kinds of products. Ask yourself who wants or needs the kinds of information that you could make available. Segment the population and then target the most likely segments. Test out your ideas with clients; let them help shape the publication by expressing what they perceive their needs to be.

Keep in mind as well that the development of a publication might have other benefits, such as establishing a relationship with a local company.

Getting Published

Suppose you have an idea for a publication, be it a professional text or lay pamphlet. How do you go about getting it published?

For a professional text, the answer is easy. By scanning the books in your office and reviewing professional journals and magazines, you could probably come up with a list of possible publishers with little effort. Virtually all will have an acquisitions editor, whose job it is to talk with people like you about their ideas. You may be asked to submit an outline or concept paper that the publisher can share internally to see if the idea fits and a sufficient market exists.

Perhaps you're concerned that if you go to a publisher, it may reject your idea and then proceed to develop it on its own. Not likely. Publishers want to encourage good ideas and potential authors. And given the fact that most educational or health professions are relatively small, a publisher is not about to risk its reputation within an already narrow market by becoming known as a pirate. If you have a good idea, put it in writing and share it with a company that has published others whose work you respect.

Researching the potential publishers for a lay publication is somewhat more difficult, in that the market of potentially interested publishers is less well defined. You may need to do some homework. For example, if you want to develop a publication for the family of a person with Alzheimer's disease, you might start with the associations or support groups that would be interested having that topic addressed, such as the American Association for Retired Persons or the National Council on Aging. You might look through the *Reader's Guide to Periodical Literature* or *Books in Print* to see who has published in this area. You might also want to contact the public relations offices of corporations that address the needs of older Americans, such as nursing home conglomerates, drug and vitamin manufacturers, and disability insurers.

Software

To be sure, the ability to develop quality software is a refined talent, and not every program is going to see software development as an attractive venture. So much the better for those programs that can and do produce computer applications that are useful and well designed.

The process of deciding in what areas to develop software is fairly straightforward, being basically an application of marketing principles. It involves answering the following questions:

- Where does the need for software exist in your field? What types of jobs that you do could be enhanced? What about in your profession (or in related professions)?
- Has someone already tried to develop such software? Is there something on the market now that would compete, and if so, could you develop something better or less expensive?
- Would there be a sufficient market? Do enough programs similar to yours have computer equipment?
- How much effort would be involved? Is the equipment on which this software would run generally compatible across various sites or would you have to produce different versions for different operating systems?
- Do you have the expertise at hand or could you hire sufficient talent?

The big question, of course, is whether there is a demonstrable need. If there is, then producing the software is basically a matter of putting together a team. This may involve writing a proposal to offset the design and production costs. It may be possible to secure equipment from a computer manufacturer, at least on loan. If you can work out the requirements, you might consider applying for a Small Business Innovative Research grant (from the Small Business Administration) to fund the development of the prototype application.

Equipment

Much of the equipment used in health care settings was designed by individuals who were trained in a particular profession but moved out of it to go to work for a company. It might be possible to put a different spin on that approach by becoming the prototype development or testing site for equipment manufacturers.

There is a facility in the midwestern dairy region of this country that could serve as a model on how to work cooperatively with the corporate sector in the development of equipment. The facility has established a reputation for expertise regarding devices that enable persons without normal speech production to communicate. Such expertise is of great value to equipment manufactuers, both in the creation of new prototypes and in field testing. It is a win-win-win situation. The companies involved have the benefit of the facility's expertise and access to clients. The facility enhances its reputation and receives free equipment as well as remuneration for services provided. And the end user—the person unable to produce speech vocally—is the ultimate beneficiary of this partnership between professionals and corporate executives.

CONSULTING

There are two fundamental reasons why a company or program would hire a consultant:

1. The consultant has *information* about a topic that exceeds its own or that is in an area it is unfamiliar with.
2. The consultant is skilled in a *process*, for example, group facilitation, strategic planning, grant writing, management techniques, or how to set up a computer lab.

Whether you are in a health or education setting (or both), your program has information to offer. The main task is to determine what information, how to package it, and for whom. You might want to start by considering potential markets for the consultative information or expertise you could provide to

- programs similar to your own in other institutions (for example, providing information on how to work effectively with low-birthweight babies)
- individuals (for example, setting up a freestanding clinic within the community)
- other settings (for example, working out contractual arrangements with local companies to serve their employees)

The "where" helps to define the "what." For example, what could you offer to a local employer? Do you know how to reduce lower-back injury? How to stimulate productivity? How to set up a performance evaluation system?

Could you offer a career counseling program for retiring employees? Or a program for expectant parents? Or a confidential counseling program for substance abusers?

What service can you offer that has value to an employer, for example, by providing a meaningful employee benefit, reducing downtime, or adding to the company's profitability?

Getting Started

In order to establish your program's consulting services, you may need to establish its credibility. You could do this by writing an article, a series of articles, or even a column in the local newspaper; providing a free screening clinic once a year; or speaking before business associations in the community. (What we're talking about here is visibility and positioning, both of which are discussed in some detail in Chapter 13.)

You may want to develop a marketing piece, a well-written letter or a small brochure that could be sent to selected businesses in your area.

WORKSHOPS

There is convincing evidence that the current interest in conferences, workshops, and other forms of continuing education will keep on. Indeed, the information explosion will only increase that interest, as will requirements for licensure and continuing education certification.

Offering workshops out of or sponsored by your organization can be a source of revenue and a way of augmenting your reputation. The usual marketing rules apply:

- Analyze the market. Who wants, needs, or would attend a workshop?
- Match the needs to your strengths. Do you have people on staff who

would be particularly good at managing the myriad details that are entailed by sponsoring a workshop? Whom do you know—on your staff, within the organization, or across the country—whose expertise would be a draw?

- Consider the appeal that your location might have to others. Would someone want to travel to your city? Are there features of the area that you could capitalize on?
- Remember that a key element of marketing is price. Although you will want to get a financial return, don't price yourself out of the market.

SOME GENERAL CONSIDERATIONS

Before launching an ambitious effort to raise fee-for-service funds for your program, you might want to give thought to the following.

Start where you are. Consider what you are doing well that could be transformed into a profit-making venture. The failure rate is highest for those who attempt to undertake business ventures that are foreign to their background and expertise—the art museum that goes into catering, for example.

Get it on paper. As in the case of any service, you will want to prepare or have prepared a formal agreement before you actually provide consultative services, and you will need to decide for yourself whether professional counsel (for example, a lawyer or accountant) is warranted.

Stay with your mission. For both tax and practical reasons, stay with enterprises that clearly relate to your program's mission.

One consideration for any tax-exempt organization that seeks to broaden its financial base is the issue of unrelated business income tax. The local Better Business Bureau may be able to produce and sell paperback books on consumer fraud and thereby make a profit on sales that is not subject to unrelated business tax. Why? Because providing such information fits that organization's purposes.

Even if business tax is not of principal concern, it should be clear by now that your program will have its greatest success when you build on your strengths.

Part III

Visibility

Communications involves an exchange between the institution and the audience. . . . To communicate effectively, senders need an understanding of the needs and wants of receivers [and to] transmit the message over efficient media that reach the target audience.

Philip Kotler and Karen F. A. Fox
Strategic Marketing for Educational Institutions

The third element of our four-part mix (the first two being planning and resources) is visibility. Visibility is more than public relations, although public relations plays a role. What we mean by visibility is the sum of all of a program's interactions with its constituencies and the image of the program that results from these interactions.

Fundamental to this part is the premise that a program can do much to influence how others view it. And as the quotation from Kotler and Fox points out, communication is itself "an exchange," as is the overall process of marketing. Marketing seeks to create an exchange in which one party offers a product or service and the other a means of purchase. Communication creates a situation in which each party knows of the other.

The second point made in the quotation from Kotler and Fox is that in order to communicate effectively, it is necessary to understand what messages will be of interest to the various constituents. Applying marketing strategy, you should consider where your audiences are "coming from" and then design your contact with them around their special needs and interests.

Much of what you will want to say will be contained within a case statement, and so this part begins with a discussion of how to develop such a document. We then move on to consider some ways in which you can get your message out.

In some ways visibility is the link between planning and development. Planning provides the what (what it is we want to accomplish). Development provides the how (the ways and means of implementing the plan). Visibility takes what's contained in the plan and presents it before potentential markets in order to encourage their investment in the program, thereby laying the groundwork for development.

Chapter 12

Building Your Case

Every cause needs people . . . for when the people are with you and are giving your cause their attention, interest, confidence, advocacy and service, financial support should just about take care of itself.

Harold J. Seymour
Designs for Fund-Raising

BUILDING A CASE FOR SUPPORT

One of the best ways of marketing your program—whether to your administration, to someone with whom you'd like to collaborate, or to a potential funder—is to use a case statement.

Case Statement? What's That?

As its name implies, a case statement makes the case for *why you*. It might demonstrate why your program merits additional staff, space, and equipment. It might explain why yours is the kind of program that others should want to be associated with. Or it might establish why your program is worthy of financial support.

In short, the case statement is a well-thought-out and carefully crafted articulation of what your program is and can become. It is the crystallization of your planning and the basis for your seeking of outside support, be it dollars, goods and services, personnel, clients, students, or new faculty. The case statement presents your best thinking, which it expresses clearly, cogently, and compellingly.

What Does a Case Statement Look Like?

A case statement might be a few pages reproduced on the office copier, a full-color printed document, or anything in between. The point is less how it looks than what it says about your program, where it's going, and why it's a "good bet."

Wait a second, you might think. If it's so important that the case statement be well designed and carefully crafted, how can a machine copy of it be good enough? Won't that turn people off?

No, for this reason: It is not essential that anyone outside your own immediate planning circle—staff, colleagues, and whoever else is intimately involved—ever actually sees the final document in its entirety. In fact, a principal purpose in developing a case statement is to provide a focus for articulating what you are all about and for agreeing on common language.

Like planning itself, preparing a case statement is a process. Although the document contains elements that you will excerpt from time to time, it is in essence a tool, a vehicle, if you will, for a program on the move. As a consequence, it might never appear in finished form. Putting it in such form would suggest that you no longer need to plan. Rather, it is likely to go through many stages, each one building and hopefully improving on previous ones.

A case statement is used in at least two different ways: (1) internally, as a means of crystallizing the thinking of those in your "planning circle" in order to be sure that you are all on the same wavelength, and (2) externally, as a means of "selling" your program to others.

Let's look at the first use. Imagine that you have laid out specific objectives that you want to accomplish. You have involved certain key players in the planning process in order to get ideas from them and to gain their support. Now you commit to writing a summary of what you want your program to become, beginning with a one-sentence statement of your perceived mission.

"Wait a second," says one of your group. "I thought we agreed to drop the idea of becoming a model outreach site in favor of having an expanded community-service role. Shouldn't that community-service role be reflected somehow in our mission? After all, that's where we're going to focus our efforts, isn't it?"

By committing the overall concepts to writing, you provide yourself with a checkpoint and ensure that in fact you have agreed to the same set of principles and to the same basic mission. More than that, it is essential that anyone whom you perceive as important to your success be able to articulate in one sentence what it is you want to become. By developing a case statement, by insistently honing the words so that there is no confusion of purpose, you will refine your mission in such a way that it becomes not only easier to accomplish but easier to explain.

OK, say you've got a good draft. Now how does the case statement get used?

- as a talking piece (for example, when you meet with your administration, with a potential staff person you're trying to recruit, or a potential investor you're trying to interest)
- in proposals to potential funding agencies

- when interacting with others whom you want to involve in your program (other departments within your institution, other community health settings, and colleges and universities you want to be affiliated with)
- as the basis for materials that you might develop or present in positioning your program in the front ranks (see Chapter 13 for a discussion of positioning)

Having agreed on the exact wording of a mission and a set of objectives, you can now commit these elements of the case statement to writing. As to the second use of the case statement (that is, the external use), you may decide, once the entire case is ready to be shared with others, that you want to present it in such a way that it can be used as a selling tool itself. If so, you'll want to consider aspects of design, layout, printing, and so on. However, you may decide to use the case statement simply as a resource, so that when you or someone involved in your program writes a memo, foundation proposal, or recruitment piece, the language is the same.

What Do You Put into a Case Statement?

In brief,

- Who
- What
- Where
- When
- Why
- How much

Who

Describe your program. Is there something in your history that would make it memorable to others? What successes can you claim? What are your major achievements? Has your program received any honors that are noteworthy? Are there persons of prominence who have gone through your program and whose names will mean something to others?

Address your program's strengths. Is it accredited by some national body? What makes it unique? What can it do particularly well? How do its goals fit the overall goals of your institution?

What

What are the kinds of things you want to accomplish? What problems are you setting out to address? What types of specific projects do you envision?

Keep in mind here that the case statement is not a proposal. Whereas a proposal might contain ten pages of copy detailing methodology for a specific project, the case statement should speak in broader terms and more briefly. It should also be careful not to presume knowledge of the topic at hand. If you are talking about a new project in the treatment of the traumatically brain injured, be sure that you use language that will be understandable not only to laypersons but also to those in disciplines other than your own.

Where

Describe your facilities in terms that emphasize what they can provide to those who use them. A set of classrooms is more than that: It's a *learning* environment. The same holds true for clinical offices. If you envision a significant expansion of these facilities (or the equipment housed within them), describe what you expect they will be able to offer in the future.

When

Provide a brief timeline for undertaking your projects. Having such a timeline is important internally and externally, as you can imagine. The timeline should reflect not only how long a particular project might take but also where it stands relative to the beginning and end dates of other projects. Is there a logical flow? Does one project depend for its success on the achievements of another?

What's the best allocation of resources? What might you accomplish early on that can be used as leverage for additional project support?

Why

Why is it so important that you undertake the work that you do? Think back to the section on planning, when we talked about describing your program in larger terms. What will you be able to do for others through the realization of your plans? If your goals seem likely to add to the image of the overall organization, it will be significantly easier to gain the kind of internal support that you need.

How Much

You've set out the history of your program. You've demonstrated to the reader that you have the potential to develop an outstanding program, one that will make a contribution to the institution, to the community, and to humankind. You've presented some very attractive, ambitious plans.

"OK," says the donor (or some other key player), "How much is all this going to cost?"

First answer: "We're not going to attempt to do it all at once. We intend to phase it in over time." (Perhaps over three years. Longer than that and most people begin to lose interest; the end is just too remote.)

Second answer: "Here's how we've costed it out."

What should you do in terms of costing it out? Provide broad best guesses estimated on the high side. Not "$79,600" but "between $75,000 and $100,000." You should also have some ideas as to where the funding might be secured. That's where developing your fund-raising marketing program comes in.

The point is that your administrator is going to panic when looking at the costs, to say the least. You need to demonstrate that you are not hoping to get the funding from the institution (at least not entirely) and that you have given some thought whence it might come.

The same is true for potential donors, even major donors. They will want to see proof that you can pull this thing off, that if they invest in your program they're not going to be alone.

Some Guidelines

Just what you say in the case statement, as well as how it looks in final form, will reflect your own style, taste, budget, and so on. But consider these general guidelines:

1. *Be positive in tone.* When you go to the race track, you bet on the horse that you think can win. The case statement is not the place to talk about how difficult it will be to pull this thing off.
2. *Be succinct.* As suggested earlier, this is not the place for great detail and surely not the place for wordiness (if there is one).
3. *Avoid jargon, abbreviations, and acronyms.* Assume you are talking to someone with a limited understanding of what it is that you do. Except for those in your own department, that is very likely to be the truth.
4. *If you do plan to print the case statement, consider how it will look.* Make it readable through the use of white space, formatting, varied type styles, and perhaps even photographs. Many design features are now possible at minimal cost through the use of a computer with desktop publishing capabilities.
5. *Think big.* The potential is enormous. You know it; here's the chance to begin convincing others.

6. *Offer a cogent argument why others should want to become involved in your program.* And don't underestimate the importance of putting that argument in human terms. It's easy—and so safe and secure—to slip into professional jargon. This tends to alienate the people you're trying to reach. Make readers feel good about becoming involved with you.[1]

In short, the case statement should present a case that is at once "rational and emotional."[2]

Who Should Write the Case Statement?

In a word: you. But who should you involve in deciding what goes into it? That requires a somewhat longer answer.

Your involvement of others in the program-planning process was carefully considered earlier. In the developmental stages of the case statement, the same care should be taken. You may want to broaden the circle of people you involve in its review while still staying with those you trust.

At the same time, sharing your thoughts—bringing others into the picture and asking for their advice—may provide an opportunity to become more visible. You'll need to strike a balance. By involving others in the planning, you increase their feelings of ownership, a positive step in getting them to feel good about your plans.

Two cautions:

1. Don't ask if you're not prepared to heed the resulting advice. If the old adage is true that you make friends by asking for help, you also make enemies by not considerately accepting help that is offered.
2. Involve others to the degree that they can help or to the degree that you need them to buy in. Some of what you develop as strategy may not be appropriate for "nonfamily" to see.

(A more thorough discussion on involving others will be presented in Chapter 14.)

MAKING A CASE FOR THE CASE STATEMENT

Just as the nature of case statements is difficult to understand, so too are case statements themselves sometimes difficult to prepare. This is not because they require great length or detail, nor is it because they demand writing craftsmanship of a high order (although they should be clearly written). The reasons are basically two.

First, there is a temptation to wait until all the plans are in place and all the bugs worked out. It's important to reiterate that a case statement, like planning itself, is a process as much as a product. Developing the case forces you to put into words, words that will be understandable to people outside your program, just what it is that you want to accomplish. Your plans will be modified from time to time, but thanks to word processors, the changes can be incorporated with ease to produce updated versions of the case statement.

Second, the uses of the case statement are unclear. "If I'm never going to show the case statement to anyone outside my division, why bother committing it to paper? We know what we want to do." Why bother? To begin with, because you can only be sure you are all heading in the same direction if you see it in print and can say, "Yep, that's what we agreed to." Print does not fade as quickly as memory. In addition, avoiding the writing may be a mask for avoiding getting underway. Writing the case statement is a way of getting "off the dime" and on with the implementation of your plan.

NOTES

1. These guidelines are in part the result of discussions with Barry Nicklesberg, Executive Director of the Funding Center, Alexandria, Va.

2. Brian Hampton, speaking on the case statement in a workshop entitled "Obtaining Major Gifts," sponsored by the Association Foundation Group, Washington, D.C., November 4, 1988.

Chapter 13

Positioning: Making Yourself Known

While Americans give away an estimated $1.5 billion annually, more nonprofit organizations face fierce competition from other institutions in the marketplace that are all vying for the same . . . dollar. The way in which a nonprofit positions its product or service and develops corresponding strategies to convey the mission to its donor base and potential markets will have significant impact on the outcome of both marketing and fundraising efforts.

Kelly A. Mahoney
"Strategic Benefits"

In marketing terminology, *positioning* is the process of getting yourself seen in a favorable context. "Positioning is not what you do to a product. Positioning is what you do to the mind of the prospect. That is, you position the product in the mind of the prospect."[1]

Positioning is achieved through a set of strategies that you employ as part of your plan, strategies that should reflect your vision of what your program can become. Do you hope to be seen as the outstanding program in your institution? As the kind of program that the institution can turn to in order to reach its own goals? Do you hope to be seen as committed to the community? As a national model program?

Positioning is another dimension in the process of thinking and acting in marketing terms. You are seeking to situate your program in such a way that it will be seen and thought of. Hopefully it will be the name of your program that comes to mind when someone in the community asks a colleague or friend, "Do you know of a good place where I can have my daughter tested? I'm afraid she just isn't picking up on reading the way the other kids did."

Developing a market position requires

- a statement of what you want to communicate about your program and to whom
- the distillation of your program's fundamental character, goals, and mission
- a brief statement of what it is that makes—or could make—your program unique (what makes the services you provide special even when others provide similar services)?

You've already done the work needed to determine your positioning stance by your efforts in planning and developing a case statement. Indeed, the case statement is worth reviewing at this point in order to come up with some brief, specific statements on the position you want to establish.

As a result of your planning, you also have some idea of how your program is perceived currently. You have baseline data against which to compare your progress in becoming not only more visible but visible in a way that helps you achieve your goals.

Developing a Positioning Statement

It is important to decide what image you want to portray and to which audiences.

You should be able to articulate in roughly ten words what you want others to think about you. Those few words should capture the essence of your program and what makes it unique. If you cannot come up with a brief statement, you may not be clear in your own mind just what image you want to project.

Try it. Ten words. Less if possible.

Shouldn't you project a different image to different audiences, for example, the community, students, government agencies, and private sector funders? Not really. Although there may be variants on the theme and you may use somewhat different words in different contexts, the message should be basically the same.

The Internal Audience

You may decide it is most important that your institution recognizes your program's promise and potential; if so, some of your positioning efforts will reflect that objective. For example, to improve your visibility within the institution, you might

- serve on committees that are of interest to the administration
- volunteer to coordinate the annual staff retreat
- help to plan and organize the tenth anniversary dinner
- offer to conduct tours of the institution

If your goal is to become known to a larger circle of potential financial supporters, your efforts will be quite different. Most of this chapter concerns how to position yourself if that is your goal.

Positioning and Fund Raising

Turning prospects into givers—that's a prime goal of developing a market position. It can be achieved through five steps:

1. Investigate how you are perceived by potential donors (or current donors, for that matter). Are there people who have contributed directly to your program whom you might contact to find out what it was that motivated them to do so?
2. Prepare copy that reflects what you want said about your program, taking into account what you have learned from those who already support it.
3. Communicate that message internally. Be sure everyone on your staff understands and uses similar if not identical language. Share that same message in communicating with other departments.
4. Communicate that same message externally by means of recruitment brochures, parent information booklets, letters, and proposals.
5. Repeat the message frequently.[3]

PUBLIC RELATIONS

"Who cares about P.R.? I'm interested in my own program and in professional publications, not in becoming a public relations hack."

Why should you care about publicity for your program?

- You have something worth selling, and publicizing is one of the best ways of getting your message out, especially to those who might support your program financially and are not likely to come into direct contact with you.
- Having some aspect of your program written about—in a mass or specialized publication—gives you credibility you can't buy. An article written about your program by someone not associated with it is likely to be perceived as objective, which can be invaluable (if the article is laudatory).

Who Gets in the News?

The *Columbia Journalism Review* examined a major U.S. newspaper to determine the origin of news articles and stories. Here's what it found: At least 45 percent of the stories in the newspaper were either reprinted exactly from public relations releases or were printed with only minor additional work on the part of reporters.[4] (In the case of trade publications, the percentage might even be higher.)

Strategies for Getting Better Known

Here are some suggestions on how you might get yourself and your program better known. The suggestions are grouped according to the audience you might want to reach.

Working within the System

It is likely that your institution has a public relations, public information, or media relations office. In fact, this office might be linked to or part of the fund-raising office. That is of course no accident: Those charged with fund raising for your institution want and need to exercise some control over how it is portrayed in the news media.

Whether or not your own public relations staff are associated with the development office, the way you approach them should be similar to the way you approach fund raisers. The public relations staff are looking for story ideas, for which you can be a source. If they find your department is particularly cooperative, your chances of getting media coverage will be greatly increased.

The reverse may also occur: No one likes to find out that another department has gone around them instead of working with them. Circumventing the public relations staff not only deprives you of their experience and contacts, it may also come back to haunt you.

The bottom line: Keep the public relations staff informed of your program, the awards that your staff have received, your accreditation by a national association, or the book you've just edited. Offer to become a spokesperson for the institution. Work together to develop a list of possible newsworthy topics.

Becoming Known in Your Community

As the *Columbia Journalism Review* study pointed out, it may be possible for you not only to attract the interest of the local press but also to influence what is said in printed articles. If you have a public relations office that you can work with, you might offer to prepare draft copy on a new venture that you think might be newsworthy. Suggest some sources that you are aware of, such as professional journals and newsletters in your field. If your organization does not have a public relations office, be sure you know what clearances are necessary from your administration prior to approaching the media.

Getting on the Air

Why should you want to appear on a radio or television talk show? For at least the following reasons:

- It increases your visibility within the community, or even nationally if you score big and get interviewed on "The Today Show."
- It can improve your program's stature internally: Appearing on a talk show may gain the attention or goodwill of your dean or administrator.
- You can parlay your added visibility into dollars by highlighting it in your grant-seeking or fund-raising efforts. Imagine how much stronger the key personnel section of your proposal on setting up a geronotology counseling center might be if you could mention that you've been featured on "Modern Maturity."
- It's one thing for you to say that you're an expert on infant feeding; it's quite another for the host of a "Nova" or "National Geographic" special to say so.

Local talk shows and national ones are constantly looking for people who can articulately discuss topics of interest to the general public. Working with the public relations staff, you might develop two approaches to getting someone from your program on the air:

1. Think about what you do that might be interesting or even provocative. What are talk shows covering in your area that relates to your program's expertise: illiteracy, hospice care, fetal alcohol syndrome, aging, marital relations, teenage pregnancy, effective public speaking, avoiding backaches? You're involved daily with issues that could be of interest to the public; don't underestimate their range of appeal.
2. Get your program listed in directories used by talk shows. For example, the *Talk Show Guest Directory of Experts, Authorities and Spokespersons* lists some 6,500 topics matched with knowledgeable persons and with programs not unlike your own. Each program can be included in up to nine separate topic areas. Surely yours could be included among one of the nine, if it isn't already.[5]

Providing a Service

Another means of getting to the potential contributor in your community is by offering a service to that contributor and his or her family. You might, for example, create a hotline that offers free referrals and responds to questions. Some hospitals have established dedicated call-in telephone numbers that callers can use to dial up information on a particular topic.

Maybe your program could launch the idea of instituting such a service. Or you might try a mini-seminar in which you offer taped programs running up to five minutes on a given topic.

The advantage of providing the community with an opportunity to call you is obvious: Those who call have already demonstrated an interest in what you can offer. If their needs are adequately met, they become prospects for fund raising.

But how do you get callers listening to a taped message to give you their names and addresses? By offering to send additional free information to anyone who leaves his or her name and address after the beep.

Set up a Speakers' Bureau

One of the problems that many organizations face in setting up a speakers' bureau is getting enough people who are willing to go out and talk to the community. Here are some ideas:

- Offer some incentive for staff to give talks, such as compensatory time off. If someone makes an evening presentation, an equivalent amount of time is deposited in a "comp time bank."
- Look beyond your staff. Those you've served—students, clients, or parents—may be excellent spokespersons and happy to give talks out of gratitude.
- Make giving presentations easy: Develop a presentation kit, complete with outline script, slides, and handout materials.

The standard caution applies here: Be sure to work within the institutional structure. If there is no speakers' bureau, create one, but do so in cooperation with your administration. You'll not only avoid conflict but also enhance your image with the institution's leadership.

Visibility in the Corporate Sector

How do you get your program better known among potential corporate funders? You start by asking yourself what they read—what publications other than the local newspaper and the *Wall Street Journal*. For example, there are trade associations for virtually every type of business, from computers to clock repair, and most publish a journal or magazine.

Businesspeople also read the publications of groups to which they want to market their products. If your nursing program wants to attract funding from Healthcare Habitats, Inc., you might do well to develop an article for your own association's publication.

Link Coverage to Funding

In Chapter 8, on private sector funding, we noted that one of the reasons companies provide financial or other support is the visibility it offers them. When you are seeking corporate dollars, remember that getting involved with you is good business and good public relations. Let the media know what you and the local gas and electric company are doing together. Not only will doing this solidify your relationship with that company, it might prompt a call from another company that is equally desirous of the image created by being associated with your program.

PRESENTING A CLEAR MESSAGE

Whether the medium chosen is print, audiovisuals, speeches, or special events, the effort is lost if the message is unclear. There are some fundamentals worth reviewing:

1. Write as if speaking to another person. You don't use terms such as *the aforementioned* when you talk; avoid them when you write. Some writers find it useful to visualize the "reader" and to consider through the eyes of that reader whether what they have written makes sense.
2. Speak to the interests of your readers or listeners. What you write or say should reflect what others want or need to hear, not what you want them to hear. One way of capturing the attention of readers or listeners is to begin by describing their interests.
3. Be brief. Even the most interesting of topics pales as time drags on.

Saying It Clearly

The following is taken from a brochure describing a university department of educational administration:

> The program utilizes an eclectic body of knowledge emphasizing a tri-dimensional view: conceptual, human and technical. This theoretical framework is a reciprocal relationship with the practicing profession which validates theory operationally and results in improvement and refinement of practice.

What business is the program in? Obfuscation? Did the writer give thought to who needed to know about the program? What usefulness it might have? How it could make a difference? Perhaps. But the result is so clouded in "philo-babble" that it is of little use to anyone outside the department itself. Will it draw students? Will it appeal to potential donors to the school? Will it help keep the department visible in the eyes of the administration?

What business are you in? And how can you state it in terms that will show that what you do makes a difference?

KEEPING THE GOAL IN FOCUS

Keep the goal of visibility in focus. It is too easy to become wrapped up in day-to-day tasks and postpone writing that article, sketching out that brochure, or launching that event. Remember that with visibility comes credibility. As your program becomes known, the job of selling it to others, both within and without your institution, will become easier.

NOTES

1. Al Ries and Jack Trout, *Positioning: The Battle for Your Mind* (New York: Warner Books, 1982), 12.

2. Norman H. McMillan, *Marketing Your Hospital: A Strategy for Survival* (Chicago: American Hospital Association, 1981), 21.

3. This list of steps for developing a market position owes a partial debt to Lindy Litrides, "Positioning Your Offer to Increase Gifts," in *The Development Chronicle* (Nashville, TN: Endata, Inc., 1988), 1–3.

4. Scott W. Tilden, "The Contribution of PR to the Marketing Mix," *Communication Briefings* 6 (December 1986): 8b.

5. Information on how to get your program listed in *The Talk Show Guest Directory* can be obtained by writing to Broadcast Interview Source, 1625 I Street, N.W., Suite 120, Washington, DC 20006.

Part IV

Leadership

What lies behind us and what lies before us are tiny matters compared to what lies within us.

Ralph Waldo Emerson

There are at least five reasons why plans go awry:

1. The planning process is flawed (for example, the strengths and weaknesses of the organization are not taken into account).
2. There is no real commitment to planning and it is treated as an exercise.
3. There is no commitment to follow-up. The process in effect ends with the plan and not with its implementation.
4. There are inadequate resources to carry the plan out.
5. The plan is sabotaged by hidden agendas.*

Let's assume that you are convinced of the link between planning and success and have (or will have) followed a productive planning process. As you set out to implement the plan, you will need to establish work plans that determine what will be accomplished, by whom, and by what date.

We have suggested some tools for implementing and monitoring plans. We have also addressed in some detail the ways in which you might garner the resources necessary to put your plan into motion. We are now about to consider the fifth factor—external forces that might prevent success.

In order for your plans to succeed, they must be grounded in reality. You need to consider what will work within your institution and how best to develop an image of you and your program as leaders. These are addressed respectively in Chapters 14 and 15.

---

*This list of reasons is partially based on a list presented by Barbara Borschow at a workshop sponsored by the Greater Washington Society of Association Executives, November 10, 1988.

Because the final section of our workshop in print concerns personal qualities that bring it all together, two points need to be made:

1. Not every leader is charismatic, a Martin Luther King whose eloquence and vision stir us all to action. Indeed, some of the most effective leaders never really appear to leave the background.
2. Qualities of leadership can be learned. Although it may not be possible to teach leadership (we can teach information but perhaps not attitudes or behavior), it is possible for individuals to acquire the skills themselves.

Leadership, like planning, is a process. Indeed, many of the same steps are involved: (1) examining strengths and weaknesses, (2) setting goals and objectives, and (3) instituting a series of activities to achieve them. As you proceed through Chapter 15 ("Taking Charge"), it might be helpful to begin laying out one or two leadership goals and some strategies by which those goals might be realized.

Chapter 14

Living in the Real World

If you have built castles in the air, your work need not be lost; that is where they should be. Now put the foundation under them.

Henry David Thoreau

In many of the exercises in this text, you have in a sense been building castles in the air—letting yourself dream a bit about what your program could become. Nothing wrong with dreaming, as Thoreau points out. Indeed, it's a very healthy activity. Try to think of one successful program that was not the result of big plans. We all have to believe in ourselves, know we're good or can become so, before we can convince others.

Now it's time to give those programmatic and fund-raising plans a foundation, a grounding in the real world. As we near completion of this workbook in print, we are going to consider not only how to get the job done but also how to deal with those forces that could shake that foundation.

PLANNED CHANGE

Developing and implementing plans is in essence creating the means to effectively control and influence change. *Planned change* can be defined as the conscious, deliberate, and collaborative effort to change a system through planned initiation of action. You are seeking to change what people know of your program and think about it. You are planning to change (for the better) some of the ways in which your program operates, for example, by improving the existing skills of staff and adding to them. You may want to alter the way in which your staff or the administration values what you do. From the start, and along the way, you need to recognize that some people view change as frightening and undesirable.

Anticipating Factors

Regardless of the work setting, before you can move from good ideas to good works, you need to think about what forces will influence your success.

Anticipating factors that may come into play involves more than identifying problems that might occur, although that is certainly part of it. It is also important to consider what exactly you want or need to change, what the vested interests and preoccupations of others are, and how to take these into account as you set about implementing your own course of action.

It might be helpful to look back at what you've said about your program's strengths and weaknesses and those of your institution. These are major factors that will impinge on the implementation of your plan.

Identifying Hurdles

What do you consider to be the single most pressing problem keeping you from making your program a real success? Make sure when you identify the problem that it relates to a goal or objective that you want to pursue. In other words, what single roadblock do you see that will keep you from reaching that goal? (*Note:* If the problem you have in mind does not relate to some stated goal or objective, that may tell you that you've missed something essential in developing your plans.)

Take a minute to articulate the problem in words that someone unfamiliar with your program might understand: "The major problem I have to solve in order to make my program a real success is . . ."

For the moment, stay with the idea of identifying the one problem that is likely to be most vexing. Then, still focusing on that one major problem, make a list of (1) those people or groups who you are confident will be of help or at least tacitly support your efforts, (2) those who may find what you want to do threatening, and (3) those who may be neither or whom you are unsure of.

What you propose to do is only as good as the support that it receives from key players around you. But who are the key players? Included will certainly be persons on your own staff, staff in other departments, the administration, board members, and so on.

Here's what your work sheet identifying those players might look like (be sure to leave room for notes under each heading).

Problem:

Key Players: **Likely Action:**
Supporters

Resisters

Middle-of-the-Roaders
or Question Marks

Briefly describe the likely action that each person identified might take. For example, you might write this under Resisters: "Dean Redpath: Will want to know how this can be done with existing financial resources. Will likely oppose the idea unless sees that it offers chance to bring in funds."

Interacting with the Various Players

How might you interact with each of the groups you've identified? In the case of supporters, be sure you don't take them for granted. What can you do to ensure they provide the support you expect?

As for resisters, is there anything you can do to soften their negative reaction? Would it be best to get their involvement early on in the hope of mitigating their resistance? Or would you do better to inform them of your plans after they are fully shaped but before you present them to the administration? (Note the implication that it may be best to inform even resisters at some point, especially if the administration will ask them for their reactions to your ideas.)

And what about fence sitters? Can you do anything to change them into supporters? Or at least guarantee that they will remain neutral?

Recognize that some people cannot deal with and will not accept any change. Whose support do you really need? In many instances, it may be someone who is not in the direct chain of command but whose opinion is often sought out and valued by those who are.

Who are the most important of the key players? Who might act as a "gatekeeper" and effectively block your efforts?

A word about making contact with each of the identified players: Be honest. This doesn't mean that you have to provide all the information you have to every person you speak with. But don't try to deceive and don't make any promises you might find difficult to honor.

Addressing the Problem

We've been considering the key players. Let's return briefly to the problem that you identified as the most pressing.

Relevant Factors

Continuing with your worksheet, list up to five factors that contribute to its being a problem. Rank each on a scale of 1–5, with 5 signifying a major factor. (Your description of the problem should be simple and direct.)

Problem:

Factors: **Rank:**

Now, focusing on the one or two factors that you ranked 5, what strategies might you develop to mitigate the problem? Is there some support that you could bring to bear that would be helpful? Is there a compromise that you could strike? Can you come up with an alternative way of getting to your goal that doesn't bring the negative factors into play?

What you should be looking for are acceptable solutions, acceptable to you and to system in which you work. There are three options:

1. You live with the situation as is. However, if you've identified the problem as a major stumbling block to your program's success, that may be an unacceptable option for you.

2. You develop a means to address the problem either head-on or obliquely. Perhaps you could get at the problem by successive approximations, living with the situation until the small changes you initiate add up to a full-fledged solution.
3. You develop a plan for achieving your goals elsewhere. If what you want to accomplish is not doable, if all the factors at work are major and you see little chance to change them, your plan needs to add a new objective at the top—finding a facility that will accommodate your goals. That may mean splitting your time between sites.

The Administration

A lot has to do with the type of administration within your institution. Which of the following six descriptions best captures the character of the head administrator?

Conservative

Likes the status quo. Has been in place at the institution a long time and wants to stay. Although not exactly resistant to new ideas, does not provide a climate in which they are encouraged and thrive. By not taking risks, is able to stay out of the limelight and safely in the wings. A survivor.

Appealing to the ego needs of the conservative administrator will probably not get you where you want to go. You need to develop an approach that does not appear threatening, that does not make the administrator nervous that those he or she reports to will want to know what's going on. Your plans, however ambitious, may need to be understated.

On the Move

The administrator who is on the move is probably aggressive. Likes new ideas especially if they enhance his or her career goals. This will not be the highest rung achieved: Has sights set on a higher position either within the organization or elsewhere. Probably relatively young for the position held. Asks tough questions.

To work effectively with the administrator who is on the move, it is necessary to consider how to present your ideas in a way that enhances his or her own apparent goals. Your program's success is a reflection on the administrator's ability to hire and manage talented people. You will surely need and want to involve him or her in your planning. To do otherwise could doom your plans to failure before they get off the ground. You may need to compromise and give the administrator a chance to influence the prioritization of your various objectives. Be sure to do your homework. Present ideas that have been given careful thought and present them well.

Business Manager

Although perhaps holding a different title, this administrator is akin to a financial officer (sometimes unkindly but accurately described as a "bean counter"). Is primarily driven by economics. What's it going to cost? Who's going to pay? Generally negative about new ideas, especially if they carry a price tag.

The fact that an administrator of this type is conservative about spending does not by itself entail lack of ambition. Rather, developing a reputation for holding tight to the purse strings may be perceived as a way of moving up. Years before he became Secretary of Defense, Caspar Weinberger was Secretary of Health, Education and Welfare. He earned a reputation for fiscal conservatism by cutting costs, holding back on funds, and trimming staff. To those whose programs were cut, he was hardly seen as a hero. But to those whom he wanted to please, he was viewed as an effective administrator.

It is possible to sell a new program to such an administrator if the program is an investment that promises to improve the financial picture of the organization.

Contented

Content with position and with the organization. Likes his or her job. Might take on additional responsibilities but will not usually seek them out. Can be supportive but will not often initiate action.

Things could be worse. Look for ways to encourage support of your plans but don't expect much more that tacit support.

The Naysayer

Always able to find a reason why a new idea won't "fly" and shouldn't be undertaken. Able to find the dark cloud that surrounds any silver lining. May be unhappy with the status of the organization but not likely to initiate change. May refer to the organization as if somehow not part of it.

This administrator is hardly the one to involve heavily in your planning. At the same time, it may well be necessary to secure at least a moderate level of support. How? By anticipating the objections that will be raised and being prepared with responses. Better yet, you bring up the objections.

Dead Wood

Every organization has some dead wood at some time. In contrast with the conservative administrator, who is a certain type of survivor, this kind of administrator holds on despite not doing adequate work. The dead wood survivor is like the student who tries to appear invisible so as not to be called on by the teacher. The student may have the savvy to raise a hand and answer questions from time to time, but only questions whose answers are a sure bet.

The dead wood administrator may not be aware of his or her ineffectiveness and may even have had some successes earlier on. That's just the problem. The novelist Graham Greene describes this kind of individual through the analogy of a leper who cannot speak and, having "lost his bell, wanders the world meaning no harm."

While being as fair as possible, it may be necessary to work around this administrator, ostensibly involving him or her but in fact getting decisions made by others farther up the chain. If that's where the chain stops, make the decisions yourself.

DEVELOPING STRATEGY

As you begin setting a course of action, you need to consider the kind of interaction you desire with the administration, your own staff, and other departments or divisions. Ask yourself the following questions: What's the best way to approach the administration? Informally? One on one? Would your approach be enhanced if you laid out an attractve graphics presentation of your plan? Is there some way you can involve one of the administrators or another key player, possibly in a joint project, in order to gain his or her support?

How can you best continue to involve your own staff? It may be worthwhile to meet with them individually to determine where they see themselves fitting in and what their concerns are. Keep in mind that your staff need to feel they have some control over their own destinies, that they do not exist simply to carry out your own dreams and plans. This is no mean trick: You want people to buy into a shared vision of what your program can become while allowing them to believe they have a reasonable degree of freedom. You don't want automatons but you do want some cohesion.

Are there elements of the plan that most lend themselves to being supported by others, that can enhance the program, further its goals, and yet not be seen as threatening? Remember that no one wants to lose status. In any change, people want to maintain their status, if not enhance it. Think about how what you are proposing will affect the prestige of other units in the institution. If you're seeking to expand your capability to provide instruction in technology, how is that going to be viewed by those in instructional technology or data processing? Is there some way that you can involve them so that they do not feel a loss of status? And if not, you'll want to be sure that your line of reasoning makes good sense, that it enhances the overall institution, that it complements an existing program instead of displacing it.

Leading by Cooperating

Zig Ziglar, who writes on the topic of success and individual and organizational achievement, points out the interrelationship between leadership and cooperation, which are both essential to bringing about planned change:

> No matter how brilliant or how technically capable you are, you won't be effective as a leader unless you gain the willing cooperation of others. For example, let's think together about the number of people you can really "force." Eliminate the boss because he is over you. You can't force those at your level because they are equal in authority. You can't even force a subordinate to obey without his filing a complaint. . . . Cooperation is not getting the other fellow to do what you want. Rather, it means getting him to want to do what you want.[1]

The operative words in this quotation are "willing cooperation." Cooperation given begrudgingly is not much better than no cooperation at all. Any problems that arise will give a reluctant partner a chance to remind you and others that he or she knew it wouldn't work and tried to point that out.

What if you are unable to establish an atmosphere of willing cooperation with someone whom you've deemed critical?

- Re-examine your own position. Is there some move that you can make that will improve the situation? What accommodations can you make in your plans that won't jeopardize their integrity and yet allow your colleague to buy in?
- Whether the individual is reluctant or willing, keep him or her informed. Nothing will turn someone from a middle-of-the-roader into an adversary quicker than the belief that he or she is being circumvented.
- Be honest. Don't tell others that you have active support from a key player when you really only have passive neutrality.
- Consider whether conditions are such that you should concentrate on a different objective, deferring one that is getting little support until you've had some success with another that may be more palatable.

A SHORT DISCOURSE ON POWER

We have been considering Change. If Change has a sister, her name is Power. In every organization there is a relatively finite amount of power, which is vested in various ways in various individuals. With power comes the ability to readily make changes, as pointed out by the "Golden Rule": He who has the gold makes the rules. Conversely, change affects the locus of power within the organization. If a particular unit changes for the better, it gains some power as a result and may move closer to the power center of the organization. As a program director, you have some authority and the power that goes with it—the power of position, of title. You may have earned some additional power by virtue of the esteem in which you and your program are held and the expertise and abilities of your staff.

We are not, however, talking about building a power base. If power comes of its own as a consequence of your success, be prepared for it. But those who seek it out often find themselves on Fortune's wheel, for a time at the top, for a time at the bottom.

What you really need is the ability to recognize where power and authority lie and to develop strategies to direct those forces. In other words, the point is not to build up power but rather to understand it and learn how to use it for the betterment of your program. What's involved? At least the following:

- Develop relationships with others. Don't hesitate to help someone else's program. Volunteer for some activity that will put you in touch with decision makers or at least make you more visible to them.
- Be well informed, for two reasons: First, because you don't want to miss out on an opportunity, and, second, because you cannot influence decisions if you are outside the information flow.
- Use the power that you have wisely and judiciously. Negative use of power will come back to haunt you.
- Work hard. "All things come to those who hustle while they wait."

A Rising Tide Lifts All Boats

Although it is true that at any given time there is a finite amount of power within an organization, it is always possible to add to the total amount of power that the organization enjoys.

Take the case of Hypothetical University. Hypo U has for years been a so-so school, posing no threat to the Harvards and Stanfords. Then one of its departments begins to develop a national reputation for work in recombinant genetics. The department gets written up in *Time* magazine and some of its faculty are invited to appear before a Congressional subcommittee. People who wouldn't have known Hypo U from Anystate College are recommending it as a place to go. And the fund raiser finds that when she calls for an appointment with the state's biggest private foundation, the response is not an automatic "Who?"

That's the message that needs to be imparted in seeking to bring about change: What is good for your program will only enrich the reputation and status of the overall institution. Think about some real-life examples and be prepared to refer to them.

It Can't Be Done

There will always be those who will come up with reasons why the plan won't work and who will offer help in the form of roadblocks. You're no doubt familiar with some of the reasons that are typically cited:

- "Let's not move too rapidly on this."
- "We need to deal with this in the context of the whole organization and the problems that it is facing; let's put this on hold until . . ."
- "Have you thought about bringing this to the Committee on Institutional Footdragging?"
- "Some awfully good minds have wrestled with this one before us . . ."

You know the individuals who are most likely to come up with these or similar reasons why this is not the time to start a new project. If you can avoid them, do so. If they are integral to the decision-making process, don't set up a meeting with them until you've anticipated the problems and worked through some potential solutions. Your best hope may be to keep them neutral so that at least they won't hold the gate closed.

Five Points about the Real World

In closing this part of our workshop in print, it's worth reminding ourselves of five things about living in the real world:

1. There are some things that you cannot change. Trying wastes energy, adds to your stress level, and diminishes your credibility.
2. As a corollary to 1: You can directly control about 15 percent of what you do; the other 85 percent is dependent on the people you work with, both those reporting to you and those to whom you report. The results will be limited indeed if you don't acquire their confidence and support.

3. And as a corollary to 2: "Dotted line" relationships—with other departments, with people outside the institution—may prove vital to achieving your goals.
4. There are some things we can change. Sometimes it is necessary to step back for a minute, maybe overnight, to put in perspective what feels insurmountable. Change is possible. Flexibility is essential.
5. Keep your eye on the goal. Even short-term failures can be useful if you learn from them and remind yourself that they are indeed only short term. The converse is also true: Short-term gains do not mean that the prize has been won but rather that you have been given a glimpse of it.

Change can be accomplished in many ways, and different leaders choose different methods. Rulers, by definition, can bring about change by willing it. Most of us are neither so lucky nor so cursed. What we have been discussing in this chapter is a leadership style that is intuitive and understated and that effects evolutionary change through insight.

NOTES

1. Zig Ziglar, *Top Performance: How to Develop Excellence in Yourself and Others* (Old Tappan, N.J.: Fleming H. Revell Company, 1986), 34.

Chapter 15

Taking Charge

Never measure the height of a mountain, until you have reached the top. Then you will see how low it was.

Dag Hammarskjold

The relationship between program success and qualitites of leadership is inextricable. It is possible for your program to succeed without your active leadership only to the extent that it is not really your program at all. It is, on the other hand, entirely possible to *manage* a successful program without *leading* it. Indeed, programs that are merely managed are probably the rule rather than the exception. And, of course, it is also possible for your program not to succeed due to an absence of leadership.

PROGRAMS AND LEADERSHIP

Three points about leadership and program success need to be kept in mind:

1. Leadership is at once the beginning and culmination of planning and effective fund raising.
2. Those programs which can be described as successful are products of individuals who exercised leadership. And leadership is evident among programs that seem destined to succeed.
3. The good news: Leadership qualities can be acquired. As John Gardner observed, "Some people may have greatness thrust upon them. Very few have excellence thrust upon them." They achieve it through "discipline and tenacity of purpose."[1]

Proud, Task, and Affiliate

A major hotel chain used to describe the three types of hotel managers that it sought out and employed as "proud, task, and affiliate."[2] Each type of manager had his or her place in the system. The proud manager, as might be surmised, liked visibility and was the first on the scene when the hotel initiated plans for a new property. The proud manager worked effectively with the local governing structure and was comfortable relating to the mayor, top business leaders, and the news media.

It was the proud manager's job to bring attention to the new property and heighten interest in the community. The job was a good fit, as the hotel chain saw it, for proud managers like being at the center of things. What was good for the hotel was good for the ego.

Once the initial phase was completed, with the construction well underway and the excitement and interest peaking, the proud manager would move on to another new property. In his or her stead came the task manager, who was good at details. There are thousands of details involved in opening up a new hotel, including details of construction, interior design, hiring and training of staff, and arranging for food delivery. If you have ever seen the PERT charts used in major building construction, you will have an idea of the extraordinary number of details. A certain type of mind is necessary to keep track of the details and manage the various activities.

The proud manager had attracted attention to the new property. Now if it was to live up to expectations, it would have to deliver. Making it deliver was the task of the task manager.

In some ways, proud managers and task managers are similar. They both like "up-front" work. The proud manager likes to establish the image early on and the task manager likes to lay out the detailed plans. Neither would want to remain at a property for years on end, running what amounts to a maintenance effort.

That's where the affiliate manager comes in. The affiliate manager is effective in maintaining the status quo—managing instead of leading. When the affiliate manager is brought to the site, the hotel is already smoothly operating; it is up to him or her to keep it that way. Where the proud manager is comfortable with the upper levels of local society, business, and government, the affiliate manager is more likely to be seen with Rotarians and the elders of the church.

Which are you, proud, task, or affiliate? Probably a little of each. If you were a dyed-in-the-wool proud manager, you probably would already consider your program a smashing success. If you were an affiliate manager, you probably would not be intrigued by the title of this book. But unquestionably there is a proud element to your character, and it is that element we will try to capitalize on in the next section.

BECOMING A LEADER

Becoming a leader means building on the leadership qualities that you already possess, reminding yourself of some truths, and learning some strategies and skills.

Lead, Not Manage

The message that leading is preferable to managing has been implicit in this chapter thus far. Let's now make it explicit. The distinction is well made in *Leaders: The Strategies for Taking Charge,* by Warren Bennis and Burt Nanus:

> The problem with many organizations, and especially the ones that are failing, is that they tend to be overmanaged and underled. . . . "To manage" means "to bring about, to accomplish, to have charge of or responsibility for, to conduct." "Leading" is "influencing, guiding in direction, course, action, opinion." The distinction is crucial. Managers are people who do things right and leaders are people who do the right thing.[3]

The implications for your own program should be evident. An ongoing program requires effective management. A program on-the-go requires leadership—influencing others, guiding the direction, shaping opinion, and steering the course of action.

Believe in Yourself

Believe in yourself. Easier said than done, to be sure. Sometimes what is required, and all that can be mustered, is the appearance of believing in yourself. Which is not all that bad: It becomes a lot easier to believe in yourself and your own leadership when it is apparent that others see you in that role. Believing in yourself implies a certain amount of risk taking: Any faith not put into practice is of little value.

You may have heard the story of Famous Amos, whose chocolate chip cookies are now renowned. When Famous Amos decided to go big time with his cookie business, he was discouraged from doing so by several friends and business colleagues. Sugar was at an all-time high, small businesses were failing (as most of them do), the economy was uncertain, and competition was keen. Friends of not-then famous Amos advised that it was a bad time to start a new venture. And for them it may have been. Amos believed otherwise and made it happen.

Lead by Example

Henry Viscardi founded his own business, a nonprofit organization that hires physically disabled workers, when he was 40 years old. Disabled himself, Viscardi was able to walk using artificial limbs, an improvement on the days when he got around on a kind of modified skateboard.

Viscardi began with an $8,000 loan and four other employees. In 20 years, he built up a multimillion-dollar organization that included a school for physically disabled children (perhaps the first of its kind in the country), a research and training institute, and an employment complex providing gainful employment to over 150 disabled persons.

He holds the distinction of being the only living disabled person to make the *Book of Lists,* where his name stands alongside those of other famous people who overcame their own handicapping conditions, such as Homer, Beethoven, and Helen Keller.[4] Although there may be numerous reasons for Viscardi's accomplishments, certainly not the least of these was that he led by example. He literally embodied the cause he expounded, both to those who supported his organization financially and to those who were themselves disabled.

Leading by example may not require overcoming a disability, but it does make some demands. What does it mean for department heads?

- It implies a certain amount of risk taking and a willingness to espouse a point of view.
- It means being somewhat proud and ready to be out in front at times. It means playing a strong role in setting the direction of your department.
- It involves articulating that direction to others within and without the department.
- It means encouraging leadership and growth on the part of your staff.
- And it means having principal "ownership" of the image, ideas, and philosophy that underpin the department. When someone thinks of the department, your name comes to mind, not just because you manage it but because you lead it, even if by letting others lead as well.

Get the Most out of Your People

A survey undertaken by the Public Agenda Foundation established what many of us have already guessed: Few people work anywhere near to capacity. For example, the survey uncovered these facts:

- Less than one out of four persons surveyed felt that they were working at the level of their real potential.
- Three-quarters admitted that they could be considerably more effective than they were.
- One out of two said that they put into their job only what was necessary to retain it.[5]

Does this sound like your staff? Does it sound at all like you? If so, how do you turn the situation around?

1. Obviously, begin with yourself. You need to inspire by example.
2. Give the credit to your people and place the blame on yourself. The Chinese poet Lea-Tse once wrote,

> Fail to honor people,
> They fail to honor you;
> But of a good leader, who talks little,
> When his work is done, his aim fulfilled,
> They will all say, "We did it ourselves"[6]

Somewhat more recently, University of Alabama football coach Bear Bryant echoed these sentiments when asked how he had been so successful. Bryant commented that if he had known any success, it was due to his players, and what failure he had known was due to himself. He imparted this philosophy to his players. When they won, he pointed out to them that it was *their* victory. When they lost, he avoided laying blame on anyone but himself. It was not a ploy, it was the way he was. It made him a leader whom others wanted to follow.
3. Communicate, communicate, communicate. According to John Gardner, communication is the single most important leadership tool.[7] Your staff needs to participate in the planning dialogue. And as painful as it may be, they are the ones who can often provide the most candid assessment of where change needs to occur.
4. Set the tone. As the head of your department, your actions are closely observed by your staff for signs as to what attitudes and behavior are acceptable. If you treat others offhandedly or are slow to respond to memos or requests, you may be establishing that kind of behavior within your program.

QUALITIES OF LEADERSHIP

In sum, it's worth remembering that leadership can be learned. You can develop those attributes that most directly correlate with programmatic and personal success. It's also worth considering these additional reminders:

- Set your own personal goals and review them regularly.
- Don't make promises you can't keep. Instead, promise less than you think you can deliver—and then provide a pleasant surprise by doing more.

- Avoid the Wallenda factor, so-called after the brilliant tightrope walker whose fatal fall to earth may have been the result not of carelessness but of thinking about falling.[8] Occasional failures are inevitable; just make the most of them.
- Feel good about yourself. Your own optimism will be infectious.

NOTES

1. John Gardner, *No Easy Victories,* ed. Helen Rowan (New York: Harper & Row, 1968), 66.

2. Appreciation is expressed to Dr. Peggy S. Williams for first bringing to my attention the concept of "proud, task, and affiliate" managers.

3. Warren Bennis and Burt Nanus, *Leaders: The Strategies for Taking Charge* (New York: Harper & Row, 1985), 21.

4. David Wallechinsky, Irving Wallace, and Amy Wallace, *The People's Almanac Presents the Book of Lists* (New York: William Morrow, 1977), 13–14.

5. Daniel Yankelovich & Associates, *Work and Human Values* (New York: Public Agenda Foundation, 1983), 6–7.

6. The quotation from Lea-Tse is found in the chapter on leadership in *Accent on Philanthropy II* (Washington, D.C.: Adventist World Headquarters, Philanthropic Service for Institutions, 1982), 12.

7. John Gardner, *Leadership Development,* Leadership Papers, no. 7 (Washington, D.C.: Independent Sector, 1987), 13.

8. R.F. Reisler, "Going out on a Limb," *Foundation News* 29 (January-February 1988): 42–45.

Chapter 16

Closing Thoughts

*Positive thinking might sound corny, but it works. It won't hurt to develop
your own personalized Dale Carnegie road course. . . . A good role model
is that hero of children's books, "The Little Engine That Could." He kept
telling himself, "I think I can, I think I can.". . . The answer to reaching
your . . . potential, ultimately, is not to anticipate disaster but to believe something fruitful will come out of your competition.*

> Peter Gambaccini
> *"Nothing to Choke about"*

If there's a theme that pervades this workshop in print, it is that you
can significantly influence your future and that of your program.

Influence comes with planning, and you're now familiar with that tool.
But planning is a little like speed reading: If you don't keep doing it, you'll
tend to slip back into old habits. You continually need to look at where
you've been, consider what you've said about where you want to go, and
reevaluate the road map you intend to use to get there. Changing your
plan doesn't mean that you haven't succeeded. To the contrary, you are
unlikely to know real success unless you are capable of adjusting your plans
as conditions change.

REENTRY

One of the difficulties in returning from a workshop or conference is
that we arrive at the office full of exciting ideas that we want to implement—
only to find that nothing has changed. Political maneuvering continues to
be a nuisance. The weaknesses on staff are as apparent as ever. Budget
forms are due Friday. Money is tight.

It helps sometimes to view the world through two lenses: a close-up lens
in order to examine carefully what is happening and to make judgments
on how to plan given the realities, and a wide-angle lens in order to see
the big picture.

You might want to jot down the four key elements that are the focus of
this book: (1) planning, (2) resources, (3) visibility, and (4) leadership.
Use the list to remind yourself that you should drive your own future, not
be driven by it.

PARTING THOUGHTS

Some parting thoughts to keep in mind as you reenter the real world:

- Build on what you can do, not on what others cannot.
- Avoid "group think." You'll know best what is best for your program.
- Feel good about yourself. Take time to reward yourself for little successes. Such as finishing this book.
- Combine vision with dogged determination.

Without vision, dogged determination is likely to get you stuck deep in mud. All the determination you can muster will not change the fact that you've taken the wrong road.

At the same time, vision without determination is little more than daydreaming. "Nothing in the world," said Calvin Coolidge, "takes the place of persistence."[1] The world is full of people with talent and education, who lack the determination to see their dreams through to reality.

It makes for an interesting combination: the letting go that is part of planning and the perseverance that is essential to hard work. We all know programs that are characterized by one or the other. Successful programs are able to combine the two.

NOTE

1. Calvin Coolidge, quoted in Lawrence C. Bassett and Norman Metzger, *Achieving Excellence* (Rockville, Md.: Aspen Publishers, 1986), ix.

Index

NOTE: Page numbers in italics indicate material found in figures, tables, and exhibits.